T0311908

Routledge Advances in Korean Studies

For more information about this series, please visit: www.routledge.com/asian
studies/series/SE0505

Strategic, Policy, and Social Innovation for a Post-Industrial Korea

Beyond the Miracle

Edited by Joon Nak Choi, Yong Suk Lee, and Gi-Wook Shin

LONDON AND NEW YORK

First published 2018 by Routledge

2 Park Square, Milton Park, Abingdon, Oxon OX14 4RN
605 Third Avenue, New York, NY 10017

Routledge is an imprint of the Taylor & Francis Group, an informa business

First issued in paperback 2021

Publisher's Note

The publisher has gone to great lengths to ensure the quality of this reprint but points out that some imperfections in the original copies may be apparent.

British Library Cataloguing-in-Publication Data
A catalogue record for this book is available from the British Library

Library of Congress Cataloging-in-Publication Data
A catalog record has been requested for this book

ISBN: 978-0-8153-9599-7 (hbk)
ISBN: 978-0-367-44521-8 (pbk)

Typeset in Times New Roman
by Wearset Ltd, Boldon, Tyne and Wear

Contents

Figures

Tables

Contributors

Jonghoon Bae is Associate Professor of Organization Theory at Seoul National University. He received his Ph.D. in management from INSEAD, Fontainebleau, France. Prior to joining Seoul National University, he worked as an assistant professor at Tilburg University, the Netherlands, as well as at Korea University. His research focuses on the network structure of exchange involving multiple persons or organizations. In particular, his research examines two related questions: coordination and innovation. The first line of research looks into the efficient structure of information flow among social actors to a given exchange to coordinate their own investments and efforts. The second line of research builds on the first line of research and concerns whether the efficient structure of information flow is instrumental to innovation by incumbents or entrepreneurial activities by start-ups. His analyses of these questions have been published in the *Academy of Management Journal*, *Industrial and Corporate Change*, and *Strategic Organization* as well as *Advances in Strategic Management*.

Myeong Hyeon Cho is associate dean and a professor at the Korea University Business School. Earlier, he taught at the Owen Graduate School of Management, Vanderbilt University, as an assistant professor. His research interests include corporate strategy and finance with a focus on corporate governance, mergers and acquisitions, and corporate restructuring. He has published numerous articles on corporate governance including the widely cited "Ownership Structure and Corporate Value," in the *Journal of Financial Economics*. Cho has served as a member of numerous government committees including the National Economic Advisory Committee, Financial Service Advisory Board, and Financial Supervision Advisory Committee. He has also been an independent board director at Samsung Techwin Corp., SK Broadband Corp. and Korea Exchange; and has worked as a consultant to SK Telecom, SK Holding Co., Hanaro Telecom, Samsung SDI, and POSCO. He holds a bachelor's degree from Seoul National University and a doctorate from Cornell University.

Joon Nak Choi was the 2015–2016 Koret Fellow in the Korea Program at Stanford University's Walter H. Shorenstein Asia-Pacific Research Center. A sociologist, Choi is an adjunct assistant professor at HKUST and was previously an assistant professor there. His research and teaching areas include economic development, social networks, organizational theory, and global and transnational sociology, within the Korean context. Choi, a Stanford graduate, coauthored *Global Talent: Skilled Labor as Social Capital in Korea* with Gi-Wook Shin.

Jaiho Chung is Professor of International Business at the Korea University Business School. His research focuses on international finance, internationalization strategy, and foreign direct investment. He received a Ph.D. in Economics from Harvard University and a B.A. in Economics from Seoul National University.

Chuck Eesley is an Associate Professor and W.M. Keck Foundation Faculty Scholar in the Department of Management Science and Engineering at Stanford University. As part of the Stanford Technology Ventures Program, his research focuses on the role of the institutional and university environment in high-growth, technology entrepreneurship. Prof. Eesley was selected in 2015 as an Inaugural Schulze Distinguished Professor. His National Science Foundation of China and Kauffman award supported research focuses on rethinking how the educational and policy environment shapes the economic and entrepreneurial impact of university alumni. Over the past three years, Prof. Eesley has been playing a growing role in national and international meetings on fostering high-tech entrepreneurship, including advising the U.S. State Department in the Global Innovation through Science and Technology (GIST) program, Chile (CORFO), Taiwan (ITRI), and the Korean Ministry of Science and Technology. He is a member of the Editorial Board for the *Strategic Management Journal*. Before coming to Stanford, Prof. Eesley completed his Ph.D. at the M.I.T. Sloan School of Management in 2009 where he won BPS Division and Kauffman Dissertation Awards for his work on high-tech entrepreneurship in China.

Jihye Kam is a Ph.D. candidate in the Educational Leadership and Policy Analysis program at the University of Wisconsin-Madison. Her research interests span the area of Economics of Education with a focus on the determinants and consequences of college-major choice. She grew up in Seoul, South Korea, and graduated with a B.A. and M.A. in Economics from Seoul National University, an M.A. in Economics of Education from Teachers College-Columbia University, and an M.S. in Economics from the University of Wisconsin-Madison. She worked for Educational Testing Service (ETS) as a summer research intern in 2011.

Sung-Choon Kang is an Associate Dean of Student Affairs and a Professor of Human Resource Management at Seoul National University Business School. Prior to joining SNU in 2008, He was an assistant professor at Korea University from 2006 to 2007. He has a B.B.A. Degree from Seoul National University and received his Ph.D. in Human Resource Management from Cornell

University. His research has focused on Strategic Human Resource Management, Human Capital, Managing Star Employees and Professionals, Compensation, Knowledge Management and Organizational Learning, and Social Capital. His articles have appeared in top HRM journals such as *Academy of Management Review, Industrial and Labor Relations Review, Journal of Management Studies,* and *Human Resource Management.* He has served on the editorial boards of *Journal of Management, Asia Pacific Journal of Management, Management and Organization Review,* and the *Korean Academy of Management Journal.*

Dae Soo Kim is professor and chair of the Department of Logistics, Service & Operations Management at Korea University Business School (KUBS). He serves as president of the Korean Production and Operations Management Society, Korea Association of Procurement and Supply Management; and is a member of the board of directors of Korea Institute of Procurement, a Korean government agency. He also serves as a member of the editorial review board of the *Journal of Operations Management,* and is a member of the Global Manufacturing Research Group (GMRG) and High Performance Manufacturing Research Group. Previously, Kim served as associate dean, executive director of the Institute of Business Research and Education, and director of Business Case Research Center at KUBS. Before joining KUBS in 2006, he was an assistant and associate professor of the College of Business Administration (1991–2005) and director of Center for Supply Chain Management at Marquette University in Milwaukee. He was also a visiting professor and joint professor at the University of Wisconsin-Milwaukee, University of Melbourne in Australia, and Yanbian University of Science & Technology in China. He also served as president of GMRG, associate editor of *Decision Sciences Journal of Innovative Education,* and vice president and director of several academic and professional societies in the USA and South Korea. He has taught and published numerous articles on operations and supply chain management and strategies, service management, technology management, project management. He holds a bachelor's degree from Seoul National University, an M.B.A. from Bowling Green State University, and a doctorate in operations management from Indiana University.

Inchul Kim is a Senior Research Fellow at the Korea Institute for Industrial Economics and Trade (KIET). His research focuses on industrial policies with an emphasis on firm productivity enhancement. His recent work includes *Changes in Globalization and Productivity in the Korea Industry and Industrial Policy Implications* (2015) co-authored with Youngmin Kim, and *The Role of Asset Tangibility on Korean Corporate Investment under Financial Constraint* (2015) with Jinwoong Kim and Youngjin Ro. Currently, he is in the process of completing a policy project for the restructuring of Korean main industries, and has started a new research project on global value chains and their implications for industrial policies in the Korean economy.

Youngmin Kim is an Associate Research Fellow at the Korea Institute for Industrial Economics and Trade (KIET). His main areas of research are labor economics, wage inequality, minimum wage, human resource policy, and productivity. His work includes *Changes in Globalization and Productivity in the Korea Industry and Industrial Policy Implications* (2015) co-authored with Inchul Kim, *A Study on Foreign Manpower Policies in Korea* (2015) with Juyoung Kim, and *The Effects of the Minimum Wage on Manufacturing and Service Industry* (2016) with Eunyoung Kang, along with publications in the *Journal of Employment and Skills Development*. He is currently researching the diverse effect of global value chains on firms' productivity and economic policies for firm stability.

Michelle Hsieh is an assistant research fellow at the Institute of Sociology, Academia Sinica, Taipei, Taiwan. She received a doctorate in sociology from McGill University, Montreal, Canada, and was a Shorenstein Postdoctoral Fellow at the Shorenstein Asia-Pacific Research Center at Stanford University. Her research interests fall within the areas of economic sociology, sociology of development, comparative political economy, and East Asian societies. Her current research explores the variations of industrial upgrading in Taiwan and East Asia and its consequences.

Hyung Oh Lee is a professor of business administration at Sookmyung Women's University. He is also the president of Korean Society of Strategic Management. His main research topics include strategy, international management, and cooperation of Korean and Japanese firms; and the vertical collaboration strategy between large firms and small and medium-sized enterprises. Previously, he was an assistant and associate professor at Hitotsubashi University's Institute of Innovation Research from 1998 to 2001; and a visiting scholar at the Reischauer Institute of Japanese Studies, Harvard University. He received a bachelor's degree in business administration from Seoul National University, a master's degree in economics, and a doctorate in economics from the University of Tokyo.

Soohyung Lee is an Associate Professor of Economics at Sogang University, South Korea. Her research area is applied econometrics, focusing on socioeconomic issues related to human capital and productivity. Her research is well acknowledged by academic and non-academic audiences. She received the 2016 Young Economist award from the Korea-America Economic Association and was selected as one of the prominent South Korean economists under 50 by ChosunBiz, a Korean news media outlet. Before joining Sogang, Lee was an Assistant Professor at University of Maryland, College Park, a Research Fellow at Harvard Business School, and a visiting professor at Hitotsubashi University. She received her Ph.D. from Stanford University and her B.A. from Seoul National University. Prior to starting her Ph.D. program, she served as a Deputy Director in Korea's Ministry of Finance.

Yong Suk Lee is the SK Center Fellow at the Freeman Spogli Institute for International Studies and Deputy Director of the Korea Program at the Walter H. Shorenstein Asia-Pacific Research Center at Stanford University. Lee's research is in the fields of labor economics, technology and entrepreneurship, and urban economics, and his works have been published in both Economics and Management journals. Some of the issues he has studied include technology and labor markets, entrepreneurship and economic growth, entrepreneurship education, and technology, education and inequality. He is also interested in both the North and South Korean economies. Lee also regularly contributes to policy reports and opinion pieces on contemporary issues surrounding both North and South Korea. Prior to joining Stanford, Lee was an assistant professor of economics at Williams College in Massachusetts. He received his Ph.D. in Economics from Brown University, a Master of Public Policy from Duke University, and bachelor's degree and master's degree in architecture from Seoul National University.

Joon-Shik Park is dean of the Social Science School and a professor of sociology at Hallym University in Korea. His research focuses on employment and regional studies. He is currently conducting several studies on the role of social entrepreneurship in creating employment and innovation. He has published several books, articles, and project reports on such issues as the impact of globalization on local people and economy; and creative innovations for sustainable local development. Park served as president of the Korean Regional Sociological Association, dean of The Institute of Global Education, and has been an active participant in academic associations and NGOs in Korea. He holds a doctorate from Yonsei University.

Gi-Wook Shin is a professor of sociology; director of the Shorenstein Asia-Pacific Research Center; founding director of the Korea Program; and an FSI senior fellow at Stanford University. As a historical-comparative and political sociologist, his research has concentrated on social movements, nationalism, development, and international relations. Shin is the author/editor of 18 books and numerous articles. His recent books include *Global Talent: Skilled Labor as Social Capital* (with Joon Nak Choi, 2015); *Criminality, Collaboration, and Reconciliation: Europe and Asia Confronts the Memory of World War II* (2014); *New Challenges for Maturing Democracies in Korea and Taiwan* (2014); *Asia's Middle Powers?* (2013); *Troubled Transition: North Korea's Politics, Economy, and External Relations* (2013); *History Textbooks and the Wars in Asia: Divided Memories* (2011); *South Korean Social Movements: From Democracy to Civil Society* (2011); and *One Alliance, Two Lenses: U.S.-Korea Relations in a New Era* (2010). Before coming to Stanford, Shin taught at the University of Iowa and the University of California, Los Angeles. He received a bachelor's degree from Yonsei University, and a master's degree and doctorate from the University of Washington.

Hyung-deok Shin is an associate professor of management in the College of Business Administration at Hongik University. He is also an active member of academic societies including the Korean Society of Strategic Management, Korean Academy of International Business, and Korean Society of Arts and Cultural Management. His research areas include business strategy, international business, entrepreneurship, and arts management. He has published papers in international journals including *International Journal of Arts Management, Thunderbird International Business Review, Journal of Business Research, Actual Problems of Economics*, and *Journal of Engineering and Technology Management*. Shin was an associate professor at George Mason University in 2003–2006, and a visiting professor at Waikato University in New Zealand in 2010.

Acknowledgments

This project would not have been possible without financial support from the Koret Foundation of San Francisco for the Koret Fellowship in Korean Studies at the Walter H. Shorenstein Asia-Pacific Research Center at Stanford University (S-APARC). Since 2008, the Koret Fellowship has brought leading professionals and scholars to Stanford to conduct research on contemporary Korean affairs, with the broad aim of strengthening ties between the United States and Korea. A major conference is held each year in conjunction with the Koret Fellowship program; in 2016, S-APARC hosted the *8th Annual Koret Workshop: Globalization, Innovation, and Culture in Korea*, from which this volume was produced. The 2016 Koret Fellow, Joon Nak Choi, is the lead editor of this volume.

We also acknowledge the financial and institutional support we received from the National Research Council for Economics, Humanities and Social Sciences of the Republic of Korea (NRC) and its affiliates, especially the Korea Institute for Industrial Economics and Trade (KIET), in organizing and executing the Workshop.

We would also like to acknowledge the support of our colleagues from S-APARC and other leading research institutions. In addition to the contributors to this volume, we would like to thank the other presenters and discussants at the Workshop, including Richard Dasher, Takeo Hoshi, Yumi Moon, Kathleen Stephens, Daniel Snider, David Straub, and Dafna Zur from Stanford University; Paul Chang and Eunsil Oh from Harvard University; Byung Chul So from the Institute of Justice in the Republic of Korea Ministry of Justice; Young Seok Oh and Do Hoon Kim from the Korea Institute for Industrial Economics and Trade (KIET); Suhoon Lee from Kyungnam University; Hogun Chang and Se Young Ahn from the NRC; Stephanie Kim from the University of California, Berkeley; Terri Kim from the University of East London; Sheena Chestnut Greitens from the University of Missouri, Siran Zhan from the University of New South Wales, and Rennie Moon from Yonsei University.

Last but certainly not least, we would like to thank Heather Ahn and Joyce Lee from S-APARC for their invaluable assistance organizing and running the Workshop.

Joon Nak Choi
Yong Suk Lee
Gi-Wook Shin

1   Introduction

Joon Nak Choi

Export-oriented industrialization has transformed the Korean economy so profoundly that it has become known as the "Miracle on the Han." In 1957, South Korea had a similar per capita GDP to Ghana, about $490 (in 1980 US dollars). In 2016, Korea's per capita GDP approximated that of Japan at purchasing power parity.[1] Unlike most other parts of the developed world, the Korean economy has grown robustly since the 2008 recession, with per capita GDP growing at a 6.4 percent compound annual growth rate. It is worth emphasizing that Korea's economic achievements have been accompanied by social achievements, as Korea scored higher than a large proportion of developed countries across many measures of social development.

Although Korea's industrial model has been successful to date, it has become increasingly fragile. Korea achieved growth through export-oriented industrialization, where the state orchestrated Korea's move into textiles in the 1960s, heavy and chemical industries (e.g., steel, shipbuilding and chemicals) in the 1970s, and electronics in the 1980s. In each of these sectors, the state selected national champions (i.e., the *chaebol*) and funneled capital into these firms. Through these efforts, the *chaebol* emerged as key actors in global markets, driving exports and economic growth (see Woo 1991; Moon 2016); in 2016, Korea is the country with the seventh largest number of Fortune 500 companies by revenue (i.e., the Fortune Global 500). Despite their success to date, the *chaebol* now face existential challenges. For instance, a rising China has produced competitors to the *chaebol*, benchmarking the Korean model and appropriating its strengths. Foreseeing this challenge, Korean policy-makers proactively sought new engines of economic growth in business services and entrepreneurship. Yet, attempts to move into business services have either failed or fizzled, and the entrepreneurial push remains at an early stage of development. These problems will be exacerbated by a demographic crisis. Decades of economic development, sex selection, and gender inequality have contributed towards Korea having one of the lowest birthrates in the world. The effects of this demographic change will soon hit the Korean economy, as the labor pool will not only begin shrinking, but also become older and presumably less productive. Taken together, these three challenges constitute a crisis, and how Korean policy-makers, executives, and civil society leaders respond to them will affect Korea as strongly over the next 50 years as the developmental state did over the past 50.

Competition from a rising China

In recent years, the *chaebol* have begun to face stiff competitive challenges from Chinese firms that have emulated them. As Chinese firms upgraded their industrial competitiveness, Korean firms have lost ground in industries that they dominated not long ago.[2] The steel industry exemplifies this trend. Much as POSCO once benchmarked Nippon Steel, Hebei Steel, and Baosteel in China benchmarked POSCO and Nippon Steel. These firms started with import substitution, largely replacing Korean imports in the Chinese domestic market. In recent years, however, they have flooded global markets with low-cost steel. In 2014, Chinese steelmakers increased their global exports 63 percent and even captured nearly 40 percent of the Korean domestic market.[3] While POSCO remained important globally, it nevertheless ranked below Hebei Steel and Baosteel in steel production that year.[4] While a surge in Chinese domestic demand captured the attention of Chinese steelmakers in 2016 and provided some relief to Korean competitors, the durability of these favorable conditions remains unknown.[5] Other heavy and chemical industries appear to be following the same trajectory. Korean petrochemical exports in 2014 declined for the first time since the 2008 financial crisis; exports into China dropped 6.2 percent from 2013 and China's share of these exports dropped to 45.7 percent from 48.6 percent, indicating a pattern of import substitution.[6] A similar pattern is emerging in the automotive industry. For instance, Hyundai has continued to do well globally but has lost market share in China, which Hyundai only recently considered a linchpin of its future growth.

In shipbuilding, Chinese firms are already posing existential threats to *chaebol*. Korean shipbuilders grew by winning market share from Japanese competitors in the 1990s and early 2000s. Around 2003, Chinese firms also began winning market share, starting in technologically undemanding segments such as bulk carriers and container ships; as of December 2015, these types constituted 66.3 percent of unfilled orders for Chinese builders. In response, Korean builders moved into more technologically complex (and profitable) market segments, including liquefied natural gas and oil tankers; as of December 2015, these types constituted 50.4 percent of unfilled orders for Korean builders.[7] Although moving into these defensible niches seemed an effective competitive response, it nevertheless made demand for Korean ships susceptible to energy shocks. These concerns materialized in 2014 and 2015, when declining energy prices reduced demand for tankers and hit Korean builders hard; in the first quarter of 2016, two of the three top Korean shipbuilders failed to book any new orders, and the third (Hyundai Heavy Industries) only booked two orders totaling US$129 million.[8] While Korean shipbuilders won Iranian orders totaling US$2.4 billion in the second quarter of 2016, Chinese firms remain a long-term threat, as they upgrade their technology and move into more sophisticated segments.[9] Indeed, of the

205,000 people that the industry employed as of 2014, about 10 to 15 percent are expected to lose their jobs.[10]

Even in industries where Chinese firms are not yet challenging *chaebol* dominance, they are still creating strategic problems. For instance, Samsung Electronics remains a market leader in smartphones, winning 23.2 percent of the global market in the first quarter of 2016 alongside 14.8 percent for Apple, and Chinese manufacturers Huawei, Oppo, and Xiaomi collectively won only 17.2 percent.[11] Chinese competitors have nevertheless disrupted the smartphone industry. Operating at low or even negative margins, they have created downwards prices pressures that have eroded profits across the industry. As Samsung slashed prices on mid-range smartphones to compete against lower-cost Chinese phones, the profit margin for its mobile division declined to 10.6 percent in the second quarter of 2015 compared with 15.5 percent a year earlier.[12] This figure nevertheless beat LG's margins on smartphones, which shrank to roughly US$0.01 per phone.[13] In semiconductors, Samsung Electronics and SK Hynix retain technological advantages and scale economies over Chinese competitors. Yet, their ongoing reliance on the Chinese market, which spent more importing semiconductors than petroleum as recently as 2013, is a real strategic vulnerability. The Chinese will invest US$161 billion into semiconductors over the next few years, and will likely generate scale economies beyond what Samsung and SK Hynix can match.[14] Overall, these competitive threats confirm Korean fears that their current industrial model is becoming unviable, and that "…an attempt to compete with China on cost or scale is bound to fail."[15] Recognizing the reality of these fears, *The Economist* described the Korean economy as "a tiger in winter" and "a once fearsome economy."[16]

A failed search for new engines for economic growth

Policy-makers in Korea have long been aware of these problems, and have sought to find new engines for economic growth. As Jung (2015) suggests, "… the rapidly changing environment has left Korea with no other alternative but to change its industrial structure." While such a restructuring has not yet taken place, it has not been for a lack of effort. In April 2002, the Kim Dae-Jung administration announced a roadmap to develop Korea into "the hub of Northeast Asia." Although the first component of this roadmap focused on the development of a logistics hub, which has proven highly successful, longer-term components of this roadmap focused on attracting multinational firms' regional headquarters.[17] This was expanded under Roh Moo-hyun to that of a business and financial hub. While advocates of this plan recognized that Korea would be competing against established financial hubs in Hong Kong, Singapore, and Tokyo in addition to a rising Shanghai, they argued that Korea had key advantages including the presence of large domestic companies needing financing, a central geographic location within East Asia, a large population with a high savings rate, and momentum for financial reform.[18] The Ministry of Finance and Economy devised a three-stage plan. In the first phase (2003–2007), it would improve the financial regulatory infrastructure, support the growth of asset management firms, and create a sovereign wealth fund using foreign currency reserves. In the second phase (2007–2010), Seoul would emerge as a financial hub specializing in the asset management business. In the third and final stage (2012), Seoul would grow into a major financial hub, with the world's 50 largest asset management companies locating their Asian headquarters in Seoul.[19]

These initiatives have unequivocally failed. None of the major asset management firms have moved their regional headquarters to Seoul. On the contrary, Western banks are retreating from Korea, closing offices established as long ago as the 1970s. Banks that have closed or sold major units in Korea include Barclays Capital (investment banking), Citigroup (consumer finance), Royal Bank of Scotland (retail banking), HSBC (retail banking, asset management), and Standard Chartered (two retail banking units). In addition to the need to react to global earnings shocks and meet higher capitalization and deleveraging requirements back home, their reasons for leaving Korea include excessive regulation and the lack of a strong economic incentive to locate in Seoul, especially in comparison with a rising Shanghai.[20] Another factor was the lack of top-end human capital (i.e., "global talent"). While Korea had a deep pool of skilled university graduates, it nevertheless faced a shortage of workers ready to function as professionals in corporate finance, management consulting, and other high-end business service roles. Reflecting this shortage, the French business school INSEAD ranked Korea only 29th out of 103 countries in the 2017 Global Talent Competitiveness Index—one rank below a less highly developed Malaysia.

Acknowledging the reality that the business and financial hub strategy has failed, the former Park Geun-hye administration shifted its focus towards entrepreneurship, announcing a three-year plan to jump-start a creative economy. Park created the Ministry of Future Planning and founded 17 incubators (i.e., "creative economy centers") that offered space, funding, and advice to entrepreneurs.[21] This approach highlights both Korea's progress and the constraints that it still faces. On one hand, state support may have contributed towards a recent flowering of start-ups, as state agencies like KOTRA and Born2Global have become "smarter and more selective."[22] On the other hand, the legacies of Korea's industrial model remain constraints. The government requested the *chaebol*, including Samsung Electronics and Hyundai Motors, to each operate the incubators and contribute their formidable resources. Their involvement, however, has raised fears that the *chaebol* would assimilate entrepreneurs into their corporate cultures, turning them into "company men."[23] Another concern is that the *chaebol* would purchase the most promising start-ups early in their development. Such a pattern would contribute towards the establishment of a start-up ecosystem by making buyouts as a viable exit strategy. Expanding this option would be especially important since only 0.4 percent of start-up founders who sold equity in Korea did so through buyouts, compared with 61 percent in the U.S. in 2013.[24] Yet, this solution poses its own problems, as the leverage that the *chaebol* would gain through their incubators might exacerbate *chaebol* dominance of the economy. While hopes remain that Korea will further develop its ecosystem for entrepreneurship, many observers nevertheless remain skeptical.

The upcoming demographic crisis

A further complication is the demographic crisis that is looming over the horizon. In 1960, Korea had a total fertility rate of 6.0, meaning that each woman was expected to have six children over her lifetime. This contributed towards the rapid growth of the Korean workforce through 2016, creating a demographic dividend: young Koreans not only enlarged the labor supply and were willing to work long hours, but also increased demand for local goods. This dividend, however, is about to invert into a crisis as traditional desires for large families have been replaced by patterns of delayed marriage and childbirth more typical of developed economies (e.g., Howe, Jackson, and Nakashima 2007). The total fertility rate, roughly the number of children each woman is expected to have over her lifetime, fell from 6.0 in 1960 to 1.2 in 2013, the lowest level among OECD countries.[25] The implications are starting to be felt today. Retirees outnumbered new entrants into the workforce for the first time in 2016, meaning that the Korean workforce has begun to shrink. As progressively smaller cohorts of individuals born in the 1990s and 2000s come of age, this trend will accelerate. As Figure 1.1 shows, Korea will rapidly transition from having a relatively young population to one of the oldest in the world:

By 2050, Korea will join Japan and Italy as having one of the highest ratios of elderly people in the world (see Howe, Jackson, and Nakashima 2007 for details).

Beyond reductions in labor supply and consumer demand, the demographic crisis will increase the dependency ratio, or the ratio of retirees to working adults. According to the Pew Research Center, Korea will have 66 elderly people (aged 65 and over) per working-age adult in 2050.[26] Each working adult will

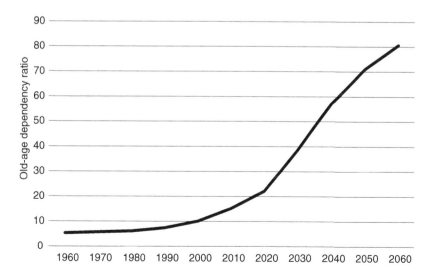

Figure 1.1 Demographic transition in Korea.

have to support an increasing number of retirees even if the retirement age is raised, straining the provision of social and medical services and creating a drag on economic growth. The age dependency ratio (i.e., the number of pension-age population (ages 65 or older) per 100 working-age population (ages between 15 and 64), increased from 7.4 in 1990 to 16.7 in 2013, with a 5.5 percent annual growth rate. This growth rate is comparable with that of Japan, known for its severe population aging (5.8 percent) but much higher than the average among OECD countries (1.5 percent). Also, the average age of the workforce will increase. An aging workforce has often been assumed to be less effective, being less responsive to changing conditions and less willing to put in long hours. Recent studies have actually found that older workers tend to be more productive, as better educated individuals tend to work longer.[27] Whether this tendency would apply more broadly to less well-educated workers, however, remains unknown. Regardless, the Japanese experience highlights concerns regarding demographic transition. Japan's population shrank by over one million from 2010 to 2015. The ratio of available jobs to applicants rose to 1.25 in 2015, meaning that 25 percent of available jobs would remain unfulfilled even if job seekers had exactly the right skills for available jobs.[28] Labor shortages alone are expected to reduce per capita GDP growth rates by 0.7 percent from 2002 through 2025, accelerating to 0.9 percent after 2025.[29]

The importance of finding a solution

In summary, the export-oriented industrial model built by the developmental state has become increasingly fragile, but its legacies continue to hinder the development of new growth engines. Meanwhile, the looming demographic transition is threatening to cripple the economy. Taking these factors together, it is no exaggeration to say that Korea is facing a crisis. How Korean policy-makers, executives, and civil society address these challenges will set the tone for Korea for the next 50 years, much as the developmental state set the tone for the past 50.

Although this volume will focus on Korea, insights from this case will also apply towards other countries that have used the state-led, export-oriented development model. While some parts of the Korean experience were unique, others were shared by other late industrializers in Asia. Notably, Japan and Taiwan have experienced painful economic slowdowns in recent years, for many of the same reasons affecting Korea today. For this reason, solutions that work in the Korean context may also work for Taiwan and Japan. Insights from the Korean case may also apply towards developing countries that have emulated its development model. Notably, China has followed in Korea's footsteps, leveraging state control over policy banks to concentrate national savings into national champions. While important aspects of the Chinese experience, including state ownership and a massive domestic market, obviously differ from the Korean one, the similarities are just as obvious. Having mastered state-led, export-oriented industrialization, the Chinese are now starting to ask where China should go afterwards, much as Korea started asking the same questions in the 2000s.

Social and economic challenges as legacies of the Korean development trajectory

The challenges now confronting Korea are legacies of strategy and policy decisions made during rapid industrialization. The Korean developmental state had great success mobilizing its initially meager resources to increase its exports. Prioritizing capabilities needed for export-oriented industrialization, however, meant that the developmental state and the *chaebol* had to de-prioritize other capabilities that were not immediately needed. The underdevelopment of these capabilities is having an adverse effect on the economy today. Figure 1.2 summarizes the legacies of Korea's development trajectory, differentiating between a *national strategy* of picking national champions, a *competitive strategy* of following industry leaders, and an execution-oriented *organizational structure*.

A *national strategy* of picking and supporting national champions with domestic savings and foreign technology produced the *chaebol*. However, this approach had the unintended effect of stunting SMEs and limiting their capabilities, as available capital and opportunities were systematically funneled to the *chaebol*. Thus, SMEs remained dependent on state support, and most exported only to the extent that they supplied intermediate components for the *chaebol*. A fast-follower *corporate strategy* was both necessary and effective for the *chaebol*, which were late entrants into markets with incumbent players. Focusing on low-uncertainty sectors where technological changes were predictable, the *chaebol* sought to catch up to market leaders and eventually leapfrog them by imitating and perhaps improving upon their technologies and designs, and leveraging their access to national savings by building large manufacturing plants offering economies of scale. A crucial enabler of this strategy was the execution-oriented organizational structures and cultures built into the *chaebol*, which quickly and faithfully implemented decisions made by the founder. The unintended consequence of this approach, however, was that the *chaebol* imprinted on this strategy and the operational characteristics implemented to support it, limiting bottom-up creativity and initiative. These characteristics have become problematic in an increasingly uncertain world where innovation has become crucial to success, leaving them vulnerable both to imitation from well-financed Chinese competitors and disruption from innovative Silicon Valley start-ups. Perhaps most importantly, *social policies* advocating conformity and rote learning produced a disciplined and skilled industrial workforce but hindered the development of the creativity and the autonomous decision-making capabilities that are so important in the new economy.

The contributed chapters in this volume trace the origins of these legacies and their contributions to the crises confronting Korea today. More importantly, they also begin to identify the strategic, policy, and social innovations needed to overcome these challenges. These chapters constitute two distinct but related sections. The first identifies the strategic, operational, and policy innovations needed to increase the competitiveness of Korean *chaebol* and SMEs. Chapters 2 and 3 focus on the corporate and competitive strategies of the *chaebol* and their close

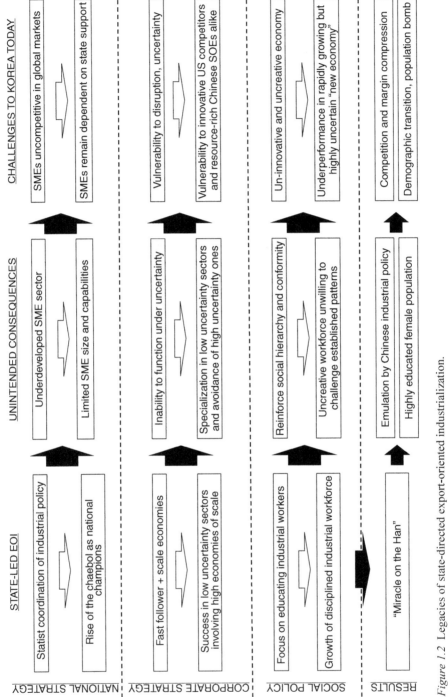

Figure 1.2 Legacies of state-directed export-oriented industrialization.

STATE-LED EOI UNINTENDED CONSEQUENCES CHALLENGES TO KOREA TODAY

NATIONAL STRATEGY

Statist coordination of industrial policy → Underdeveloped SME sector → SMEs uncompetitive in global markets

Rise of the chaebol as national champions → Limited SME size and capabilities → SMEs remain dependent on state support

CORPORATE STRATEGY

Fast follower + scale economies → Inability to function under uncertainty → Vulnerability to disruption, uncertainty

Success in low uncertainty sectors involving high economies of scale → Specialization in low uncertainty sectors and avoidance of high uncertainty ones → Vulnerability to innovative US competitors and resource-rich Chinese SOEs alike

SOCIAL POLICY

Focus on educating industrial workers → Reinforce social hierarchy and conformity → Un-innovative and uncreative economy

Growth of disciplined industrial workforce → Uncreative workforce unwilling to challenge established patterns → Underperformance in rapidly growing but highly uncertain "new economy"

RESULTS

"Miracle on the Han" → Emulation by Chinese industrial policy → Competition and margin compression

Highly educated female population → Demographic transition, population bomb association with their operational processes and business cultures; Chapters 4 and 5 shift their focus towards Korean SMEs and policy infrastructure supporting them. These four chapters not only highlight a need for firm-level strategic and operational innovations, but also policy and social innovations to enable these firm-level innovations. The second section (Chapters 6 through 9) examines how Korea might leverage its growing diversity and openness to outsiders to generate the capabilities needed for the firm-level innovations discussed in the first section.

The need for strategic and operational innovation by the chaebol

The national strategy of achieving late industrialization through export-oriented industrialization, as orchestrated by the developmental state, culminated in the rise of the *chaebol* as externally competitive national champions. This strategy has bestowed powerful legacies on *chaebol* strategy and organization. The *chaebol* no longer depend on state support for their core products, and have their own strategic and analytical capabilities. Thus, they typically make decisions independently of state-led directives, based mostly on their perceptions of market trends.[30] Yet, the legacies of state-led development have remained imprinted on the way the *chaebol* make strategic decisions and conduct operations. During the heyday of the developmental state, the Economic Planning Board and other state agencies largely determined *corporate strategy* regarding what industries the *chaebol* entered and their mode of entry. State agencies, however, had less say over *competitive strategy*, on the way the *chaebol* would compete against rivals in an industry once they had entered, and the *operations* implementing this strategy. Nevertheless, state-led development had an indirect effect on competitive strategies and organizational structures. The *chaebol* were thrust into industries that already had incumbent players. To unseat these market leaders, the *chaebol* had little choice other than to adopt a fast-follower strategy and related organizational structures and operational templates, benchmarking industry incumbents before leaping ahead of them using scale economies made possible by the financial resources provided by the developmental state and internal capital markets. As organizations generally tend to do, the *chaebol* imprinted on these conditions, retaining a *modus operandi* optimized for these conditions even after they had outgrown them.[31] Even though many *chaebol* have become industry leaders, they generally continue to avoid being first movers into new opportunities, preferring to be fast-followers once the first mover has defined a market segment and resolved the uncertainties found there.

Chapter 2 examines the corporate strategies that the *chaebol* have used to compete against Japanese and Chinese rivals in the electronics industry. Authors Hyung Oh Lee and Hyung-deok Shin are professors of business strategy at leading Korean business schools; Lee is also the president of the Korean Society of Strategic Management. Their study decomposes corporate strategy into several parts. Global strategy, or the choice of foreign markets in which to operate, has been a key advantage for the *chaebol* over Japanese competitors.

Paradoxically, the large and stable Japanese home market has encouraged Japanese firms to focus on this market and avoid foreign markets, while the relatively smaller Korean market has forced the *chaebol* to expand and thrive in global markets. Lee and Shin propose that the *chaebol* would benefit by further globalizing their sales, production, and administrative functions such as research and development. Diversification strategy, or the choice of market segments, has also given the *chaebol* an advantage over Japanese competitors. The crucial change has been a shift from integral production, where non-standard components must be tightly and idiosyncratically integrated, to modular production, where highly standardized components can simply be mashed together. While this shift enabled less-experienced Korean firms to compete against established Japanese competitors, it has also negated the experience advantage that Korean firms have relative to up-and-coming Chinese firms. Vertical integration, or sourcing parts internally rather than externally, is an approach that is shared by the *chaebol* and Japanese competitors, while Chinese firms tend to be more open to outsourcing. Such openness is a potential competitive advantage for the Chinese, especially if externally sourced parts can be integrated as modules. Overall, this chapter highlights the strategic rationales for the *chaebol* to enter new international markets and industry segments, but also that the *chaebol* cannot do so without developing capabilities to better leverage foreigners and work with external partners.

Chapter 3 shifts its focus towards competitive strategy, examining how the *chaebol* have imprinted upon developmentalist legacies, and how this has constrained their competitiveness. Lead author Myeong Hyeon Cho and his collaborators are professors at leading Korean business schools. According to their chapter, the *chaebol* have maintained organizational structures and cultures, human resources practices, and operations that support a fast-follower strategy. Control remains concentrated in the hands of the founder or his heirs, facilitating the redeployment of capital from one large-scale investment to another according to his (or her) strategic directives. However, the fear of losing control causes chairpersons to avoid emerging sectors characterized by high uncertainty. Also, the *chaebol* rely on informal internal networks among employees embedded into the same corporate culture, leaving core processes underdocumented. While this *modus operandi* has been excellent for cutting through bureaucracy to speedily execute the chairperson's directives, it hinders attempts to work with external partners or conduct mergers and acquisitions; a reliance on shared corporate culture rather than documented formal processes makes it difficult for outsiders to understand how things are done, as informal culture is far more opaque to outsiders than formal processes. In terms of human resource management, the *chaebol* rely on internal labor markets and promotions, separating insiders from outsiders. While this approach has increased trust among core *chaebol* employees, increasing execution speed and efficacy, it has also hindered them from accepting knowledge from sources external to the organization. Together, these limitations force the *chaebol* to rely upon a few close partners that understand their unique cultures and informal processes, preventing the *chaebol* from broadening their supply chains to reduce cost and improve quality. Overall, this chapter proposes that the organizational structures, human resources practices, and supply chains that had been so effective at pursuing a fast-follower strategy have become maladaptive and require substantial reform.

These chapters look backwards to explain why the *chaebol* have adopted their strategies and operational processes, but also look forwards to highlight the threats they are facing and the reforms that they will need to adopt in the face of rising Chinese competition. Constrained from globalizing and expanding into emerging market segments more intensively, and locked into a fast-follower competitive strategy and operational processes, the *chaebol* are now vulnerable to both Chinese imitators that combine a fast-follower strategy with economies of scale and Silicon Valley innovators that disrupt established industries to create a niche for themselves. Lee and Shin suggest corporate strategy innovations to counter these threats, including more intense globalization and entry into emerging, dynamic market segments. Yet, as Cho et al. emphasize, the *chaebol* remain imprinted upon the legacies of the developmental state, and lack the ability to follow Lee and Shin's suggestions by evaluating emerging opportunities in dynamic markets, leveraging foreigners and their resources, and interfacing with external partners. The final point is particularly important as a large body of research in organizational theory has demonstrated that networks of partnerships are ideal for dealing with uncertainty.[32] Overall, the lack of capabilities for functioning in an increasingly uncertain and globalized world has prevented the *chaebol* from achieving even greater success in global markets.

The need for SME policy innovation

An unintended consequence of the developmental state picking national champions has been the underdevelopment of the SME sector. During the 1960s, the state privileged the *chaebol* over the SMEs. The dominant literature attributes control of finance as the key element of the Korean developmental state (e.g., Woo 1991), and attributes the weakness of the SME sector to the lack of capital. The developmental state, however, also procured foreign technologies on behalf of the *chaebol* and preferentially provided them with export licenses. Furthermore, the government allowed *chaebol* to import intermediate components duty-free, hoping to capture the value added from assembling these components into finished products that would then be exported. Such policies had profound impacts on the development of the SMEs. The immediate consequences of the export promotion policies, such as the creation of generalized trading companies (i.e., internal capital markets) and industrial targeting in the 1970s, were that the *chaebol* actively diversified and expanded into areas in which they were not initially specialized, acquiring SMEs across diverse businesses to reach export targets and the requirement of diversification of export items established by the state (Lim 1997, 141; Choi 1993, 38–39). Over time, these factors led to the concentration of trading knowledge and overseas market information in the hands of a few large *chaebol*. Facing limited trading channels the surviving Korean SMEs remained dependent on the *chaebol* for technology, foreign sales, and capital.

An important consequence of the initial underdevelopment of the SME sector has been the ongoing importance of government support. In the economy as a whole, the developmental state has largely faded away during the past few decades, as Korea has democratized and begun conforming to global market-oriented standards.[33] Indeed, healthy *chaebol* have largely made strategic decisions based largely on global market trends, although state-led directives continue to have salience especially for financially strained *chaebol*. In contrast, the SMEs developed neither the strategic nor operational capabilities needed to operate independently, and continue to depend on state support. Starting in the 1980s, the state began to recognize the need to reduce intermediate component imports by supporting SMEs, and began to provide tax incentives and financial support. In the 1990s, the state further recognized that technology start-ups could contribute greatly towards economic growth, and aggressively sought to remove obstacles to the formation and growth of these SMEs. Such factors remain especially important as SMEs (i.e., enterprises with fewer than 300 employees) constitute 99 percent of all firms in Korea and account for 87.7 percent of total employment in the economy as of 2012 (SBC publication). Chapters 4 and 5 of this volume focus on policies intended to remediate the historical underdevelopment of the SME sector, the need to reform these policies, and for the SMEs themselves to adopt strategic innovations and build their own operational capabilities.

Chapter 4 highlights export promotion in the SME sector as a legacy of Korea's state-centered development trajectory. Authors Inchul Kim and Young-min Kim are research fellows at the Korea Institute for Industrial Economics and Trade specializing in industrial economics. They argue that given the relatively small size of the Korean domestic market, a key prerequisite to the growth of Korean SMEs is expansion into global markets. SMEs, however, lack many of the basic capabilities needed to enter foreign markets, including information about these markets. Recognizing these problems, the state has created an export promotion framework reminiscent of the developmental state in the SME sector, setting quantity-driven export targets. Kim and Kim show that the Korean state has provided a great deal of export promotion support for its SMEs, spending more per capita supporting SMEs than any other country in the world. Despite such support, few Korean SMEs survive in global competition, reflecting their dearth of global capabilities and the ineffectiveness of export promotion policies. Kim and Kim, however, find a silver lining. The few Korean SMEs that survived for three years in global markets accelerated their growth rate, demonstrating that it is possible for SMEs to build the capabilities needed to succeed overseas on their own with enough perseverance.

Chapter 5 investigates how the Korean government adopted cluster-oriented development to support SMEs, and how these efforts have replicated the pattern of creating national champions. Author Michelle Hsieh is a research fellow at Academia Sinica in Taiwan, and has intensively examined innovation and cluster-oriented development in the Asian context. Cluster-oriented economic development is the idea that geographically co-located SMEs can generate new capabilities and competitive advantages by partnering with each other. As practiced in Taiwan and elsewhere, the government plays a key role in this process, facilitating horizontal connections among peer SMEs. While the government also plays a key role in Korea, it has encouraged vertical ties linking SMEs with the state instead of horizontal ties among SMEs, replicating the production of national champions on a smaller scale by creating an infrastructure for selecting and nurturing specific SMEs but not others. Hsieh largely attributes the failure of cluster-oriented development in Korea to this tendency.

These chapters highlight the continued dependence of Korean SMEs on forms of state support that remain highly influenced by the developmental state, and the ineffectiveness of this continuing pattern. Both chapters highlight the need for policy reform in the SME sector and the need for SMEs to build their own capabilities instead of relying on state support. How SMEs might acquire key capabilities, including the ability to cooperate across organizational and national boundaries and to innovate, forms the focus for later chapters in this volume.

The need for social change to create economic capabilities

The policy, strategy, and operational innovations proposed in the chapters as described above are necessary but perhaps insufficient to overcome the challenges faced by Korea. Chapters 2 through 5 not only identify crucial ways in which state policy and corporate strategy and operations should be reformed, but also missing capabilities needed to implement such innovations. One of the key contentions of this volume is that *social innovation* can provide these capabilities and bestow economically important capabilities on SMEs and the *chaebol* alike.

The resource-based view (i.e., RBV), a popular approach to analyzing business strategy, is useful for exploring this possibility. According to this view, a firm's competitive advantages are based on the *resources* and *capabilities* that it controls. Resources include natural resources such as steel deposits, and tools such as factories, and the specialized expertise constituting human capital. Capabilities are resources that enable other resources to be used more effectively, such as managerial effectiveness. Thus, capabilities multiply the competitive effectiveness of an item or group. While all capabilities are important, attention has shifted away from *operational capabilities* enabling firms to maintain the status quo towards *dynamic capabilities* enabling firms to adapt to a changing environment by building, integrating, or reconfiguring operational capabilities. Part of the reason why dynamic capabilities have taken on greater importance is because globalization and technological change have increased complexity and uncertainty across world markets. Indeed, dynamic capabilities are particularly important in knowledge-intensive new economy sectors such as the Internet and mobile application development.[34] Chapters 2 through 5 suggest that Korean SMEs and *chaebol* are missing some of the dynamic capabilities needed for the policy, strategy, and operational innovations that they prescribe. The *chaebol* already have one important dynamic capability, the ability to imitate and improve on first movers' products.[35] Whenever a market leader introduces a new product, a *chaebol* can eliminate any competitive disadvantages by quickly introducing an upgraded version. Nevertheless, having the ability to catch market leaders does not necessarily equate to the ability to lead the market. Together, Chapters 2 through 5 identify three missing dynamic capabilities—the *creativity* and the ability to *cooperate with external actors* needed to disrupt incumbent market leaders and to respond to disruptions themselves, and the ability to *leverage foreigners* and their skills and knowledge to gain a full understanding of foreign markets and consumers. A large literature in sociology and management research has linked these dynamic capabilities with social networks and social norms on the way individuals should function within these networks.

Social structure and dynamic capabilities

Creativity and its application to practical problems—innovation—usually results from the social context. Creativity can be described as a process of recombining distinct and disparate forms of knowledge.[36] Contrary to popular belief, creativity seldom results from individual genius, but rather from individuals being exposed to different contexts and transposing concepts across them.[37] For example, Apple gained a reputation as an innovator with the Macintosh, which was one of the first computers to use a graphical user interface where users issued commands by moving a cursor around the screen and clicking on icons representing files or programs. While many credited the individual genius of CEO Steve Jobs for producing the Macintosh, Jobs had actually licensed the technology from another company. What made the Macintosh a success were the incremental innovations that Jobs and Apple incorporated into it, such as the ability for users to specify fonts. Jobs later described the process by which he generated this innovation:

> Reed College ... offered perhaps the best calligraphy instruction in the country. Throughout the campus every poster, every label on every drawer, was beautifully hand calligraphed. Because I had dropped out and didn't have to take the normal classes, I decided to take a calligraphy class to learn how to do this. I learned about serif and sans serif typefaces, about varying the amount of space between different letter combinations, about what makes great typography great. It was beautiful, historical, artistically subtle in a way that science can't capture, and I found it fascinating.... None of this had even a hope of any practical application in my life. But 10 years later, when we were designing the first Macintosh computer, it all came back to me. And we designed it all into the Mac. It was the first computer with beautiful typography. If I had never dropped in on that single course in college, the Mac would have never had multiple typefaces or proportionally spaced fonts.[38]

Diversity drives the potential for innovation by exposing individuals to different contexts. The co-location of unrelated activities enhances creativity and innovation by creating opportunities for transposing practices and their underlying logics across these activities.[39] Similarly, social proximity creates opportunities for creativity, especially when multiple logics (i.e., justifications) are present within an industry or field. When established ideas are widely taken-for-granted, they are rarely challenged, and thus pose a barrier for creativity and innovation.[40] For this reason, industries or fields with multiple, competing logics and practices tend to have the greatest levels of creativity and innovation.[41]

Social networks have been found to play an especially important role in these processes. Even if diverse actors are co-located or are performing the same activities, they do not always interact with each other. Whether such interactions will occur depends largely on social network structure (Figure 1.3). A large literature theorizes social networks as being closed or open. Closed networks consist of homogeneous groups of individuals linked by strong ties, while open networks are characterized by weak-tie bridges across different groups. Most networks feature both closure and openness, varying in the degree to which bridges link groups together.

This model represents an ideal-type structure, and its assumptions are almost always violated in some way. Yet, the model is useful for theorizing how network structure affects creativity and innovation. Cross-cutting bridges (i.e., brokerage) are useful for gaining access to new ideas and practices, as they connect diverse groups together. As heterogeneity tends to weaken trust within social ties and decrease the frequency of interaction, bridges tend to be weak

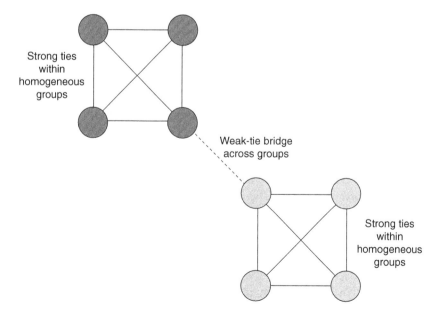

Figure 1.3 Ideal-type social network structure showing brokerage and closure.

ties.[42] However, closure can also be useful, with the strong ties found within closed groups enabling individuals to exploit innovations.[43] For these reasons, empirical research suggests that individuals who are simultaneously embedded in closed groups through their strong ties and connected to outsiders through their weak ties tend to be the most successful innovators.[44] Recent studies have found that the social norms governing interactions in social networks matter as much as the structure of the networks themselves. The importance of weak-tie bridges is that they spread new ideas and practices from diverse sources across the network as a whole. Yet, the salience of weak ties varies across cultures. For instance, weak-tie bridges do not function in Asian societies as they do in the USA. Where group-oriented collectivist identities and within-group bonding are especially powerful, weak-tie bridges appear to lose their salience.[45]

The same factors also affect the ability to work with outsiders. Social networks consist of trust relationships that facilitate interaction and cooperation.[46] Consequently, weak-tie bridges matter greatly for cooperation between individuals across different groups and organizations, who often need a reason to trust each other.[47] The presence of bridges is necessary but not sufficient, however, as the cultural context also matters. Individuals in contexts where they are encouraged to reach out to outsiders and learn from them (i.e., polyculturalism) would be more likely to do so, not only building bridges but also using them. Conversely, individuals in contexts where outsiders are distrusted and largely avoided, which is often the case in collectivist societies, will avoid using even the bridges they had previously built. Overall, exclusionary norms relating to collectivism should negatively moderate the effect of weak-tie bridges in facilitating inter-group or inter-organizational cooperation.

Likewise, social network structure and the norms governing interactions within networks should also affect an actor's ability to deal with uncertainty. Individuals and organizations can deal with uncertainty *ex ante* by collecting and processing information that can help them predict future events. Once such predictions are made, individuals and organizations can formulate strategic or operational responses. In this context, social networks represent potent information collection and processing tools, leading to better predictions.[48] Individuals and organizations can alternatively deal with uncertainty *ex post*, reacting to unexpected events by mobilizing the resources found within their networks. The trust and flexibility embodied by networked forms of organization helps actors respond quickly and effectively.[49] For both *ex ante* and *ex post* reasons, social network structures rich in weak-tie bridges, and also embodying social norms encouraging the activation of these bridges, should help individuals and organizations cope with uncertainty better.

These theoretical insights suggest an explanation why Korean firms are largely unable to be creative, work with outsiders or deal effectively with uncertainty. Although Korean society is rapidly changing, it remains characterized by a strong collectivist orientation at three levels of analysis. Koreans tend to subordinate their individual needs and aspirations to those of their families, although this tendency has possibly weakened in recent years. Koreans are also oriented towards the organizations in which they are members, especially to their work-places and educational institutions. This orientation is so strong that it nearly matches their orientation towards their families in strength.[50] Finally, Koreans remain oriented towards their shared ethnic identity, and retain their tendency to exclude outsiders.[51] These three forms of collectivism not only discourage the formation of weak-tie bridges outside their own families and organizations as well as the Korean ethnicity, but also dissuade existing weak-tie bridges from being activated. Thus, they tend to stifle creativity, increase the difficulty of cooperating with partners external to the group, organization, or the nation, and deal with uncertainty either *ex ante* or *ex post*.

These tendencies have been further exacerbated by the legacies of the developmental state. Korea's developmental experience was nothing less than a total social mobilization to create a disciplined and skilled industrial workforce, with the unintended consequence of suppressing other crucial skills needed for a post-industrial economy. One of the key social initiatives associated with the developmental state was to enhance the educational system, first by expanding primary education to produce workers for light industry in the 1960s, then by expanding secondary education to produce workers for the heavy and chemical industries in the 1970s and 1980s, and finally by expanding tertiary education in the 1990s. Especially in the first two stages, the state adopted lecture-based rote memorization, as the most efficient way to train basic skills to a large number of students given a limited number of teachers.[52] The state also enforced discipline in society, starting with mandatory military service and reinforced by military-like workplace patterns. Even the Saemaul movement involved the teaching of discipline through the "spiritual training" of rural farmers.[53] Beyond strengthening existing collectivist tendencies, the unintended consequence of creating such an industrial workforce has been the difficulty of transforming that workforce into a post-industrial one. Although Korea has greatly increased its proportion of college graduates, consistently awarding college degrees to either the highest or the second highest proportion of individuals born in recent years, it has yet to produce creative individuals capable of independent decision-making in the large numbers needed by a post-industrial economy. A large problem is a curriculum in primary and secondary educational institutions that continues to highlight rote learning. While this was ideal for training industrial workers to execute top-down directives, it has proven counterproductive for training post-industrial workers to analyze complex systems and make autonomous decisions. Largely for these reasons, along with the effects of mandatory military service and a collectivist cultural heritage, Korean workers tend to look towards their seniors for guidance rather than attempting to solve problems and resolve conflicts on their own. Overall, the Korean workforce has remained somewhat uncreative, unwilling to challenge established patterns and reliant on particularism and ethnic nationalism as sources of solidarity.

The central argument made by the second half of this volume is that Korea can develop missing capabilities by embracing increased gender and ethnic diversity. The basic idea is that social networks that encompass more diversity, given a culture of accepting such diversity, tend to facilitate creativity and have the collective capacity to absorb new ideas and innovations. Thus, individuals embedded in these networks will have better capabilities for transposing or combining ideas across fields, and working with those from outside their organizational or national cultures. Should these capabilities become widespread within Korean society—in other words, increasingly characterize individuals and groups within Korean society—SMEs and the *chaebol* can leverage these capabilities by hiring individuals with these skills and mindsets.[54]

While Korea is sometimes stereotyped as a sexist and xenophobic society, two of the most salient trends in Korea today are increasing gender equality and greater social acceptance of non-Koreans. There is no doubt that gender inequality continues to be a major problem in Korean society. Korea continues to have the highest gender wage gap in the OECD, with males making 36.6 percent more than women in the same workplace roles.[55] The pattern of female labor force participation has been M-shaped, with women working at high rates early and late in their lives, but not during their childrearing years. Indeed, nearly two out of five married women quit their jobs after marriage, prioritizing childrearing, education, and other family-related obligations.[56] Yet, gender inequality has nevertheless been diminishing rapidly in recent years. For instance, the number of women working in local governments increased by 83.3 percent over the past two decades, accounting for more than half of new hires since 2005. Furthermore, the number of women in managerial positions increased 419.7 percent during the same time period.[57] In the private sector, 56,000 women worked for the Samsung Group in 2012, a quarter of its total workforce. This number includes three women who were promoted into executive roles for the first time; Samsung's other 31 female executives had been hired externally rather than promoted from within. Still, the proportion of female executives remained at only 2 percent, far below the proportion found in comparably large US firms.[58] Likewise, Korea remains strongly ethnic nationalist, which has hindered the country's ability to recruit skilled foreigners and even members of the diaspora.[59] Korea remains somewhat intolerant of those who are not ethnically Korean. However, the trend has been towards greater acceptance. For instance, the proportion of Koreans who distrust foreigners living in Korea decreased from 72.9 percent in 2005 to 68.0 percent in 2010.[60] As these trends indicate, a Korea that embraces gender and ethnic diversity has entered the realm of realistic possibility, given ongoing social changes. The second half of this volume focuses on sources of increased gender, ethnic and geographic diversity.

Accelerating the entry of women into the workplace

Chapter 6, authored by economists Jihye Kam and Soohyung Lee who have studied demographic trends, examines how a trend towards gender equality can be leveraged by investigating how the choice of college majors hinders the entry of women into the workforce and how it might be remediated. Beyond enhancing firms' creativity and absorptive capacity, the entry of women into the workforce helps alleviate the effects of the demographic crisis by replenishing the labor pool.[61] This chapter examines how a factor that is not directly related to gender discrimination, the choice of college major, accounts for about half of the gender gap in earnings and employment. While men are more likely to major in engineering, which offers good career prospects, women are more likely to select humanities and arts/athletics majors that offer poor career prospects. Kam and Lee conduct a thought exercise, to see how nudging women into science, technology, engineering, and mathematics (STEM) fields might increase their workforce participation and earnings, and magnify the benefits gained from the ongoing trend of increased gender equality.

Accelerating the benefits of globalization

While gender represents a source of diversity within the traditional notion of the Korean nation, globalization represents a source of diversity beyond these boundaries. An inflow of individuals with international exposure, whether or not they are ethnic Koreans, increases the diversity of backgrounds, skills, and information available to the *chaebol* and SMEs alike. The following chapters show that Korea can build a global outlook and grow more creative and entrepreneurial, but only if outsiders are incorporated into Korean society and economy in a meaningful way.

Chapter 7 examines Korean nationals studying abroad as a source of diversity, especially regarding knowledge of global contexts and new innovations. Authors Joon Nak Choi and Chuck Eesley are, respectively, a sociologist focusing on global connections and a management scholar focusing on entrepreneurship and innovation. They argue that policy-makers, executives, and the media have long been concerned about the brain drain, which occurs when talented Koreans study abroad and remain in their host countries, contributing their talents and skills there instead of returning home. In recent years, discussions of study abroad have broadened to encompass the possibility of brain circulation, which occurs when students remain abroad and build their human and social capital in the workplace before bringing these resources back to Korea. Such brain circulation is especially potent as individuals often maintain their connections with both Korea and their host countries, magnifying the creativity and absorptive capacity benefits of embedding them back into Korean society. What has yet to be discussed, however, is the possibility of brain linkage, where students remain abroad permanently but nevertheless maintain ties and funnel resources back into Korea. This chapter examines the conditions under which brain drain, circulation, and linkage occur among Korean graduates of Stanford University, and finds that students are more likely to return home if they completed their undergraduate studies in Korea before heading abroad, and if they studied in fields where Korea offers adequate or perhaps even superior job prospects. This chapter also provides concrete but limited evidence of brain linkage, in the form of Koreans who remained overseas, yet provided funding and advice for Korean start-ups. Overall, this chapter illustrates how Korean students overseas can increase the diversity of the Korean workforce.

Chapter 8 highlight the limits of the phenomenon discussed in Chapter 7, however. Lead author Yong Suk Lee is an economist focusing on innovation and entrepreneurship. Along with co-author Chuck Eesley, he examines the degree to which Koreans and other Asians who studied abroad at Stanford University absorbed entrepreneurial values. Despite Stanford being located in Silicon Valley and being considered the pre-eminent institution for teaching and disseminating entrepreneurial values, this chapter finds that Koreans and other Asians who studied there do not become substantially more entrepreneurial, even though Korean Americans and other Asian Americans do become substantially more entrepreneurial in the same environment. This finding suggests that there are limits on relying on Korean nationals as a source of global diversity, necessitating that individuals who are further removed from the Korean context and socialized elsewhere (i.e., members of the diaspora or even true foreigners) be recruited as a source of diversity.

Chapter 9 (Park) synthesizes the propositions of the first and second halves of the volume, showing how national diversity and an appreciation for such diversity enabled the *chaebol* to enter and adapt to the Chinese marketplace. Author Joon-Shik Park is a sociologist who has spent a substantial amount of time studying Korean firms in China. Over a million ethnic Koreans who lived in China, and have nearly completely adapted to the environment there, have either returned to Korea in search of economic opportunities or have begun working for the *chaebol* in China. Functioning as "human brokers" bridging Korean firms and the Chinese host environment, the Korean Chinese played a crucial role in the initial stages of successful entry of the *chaebol* into Korea, helping them navigate relationships with government officials and other culturally specific hurdles. In this process, many Korean Chinese rose to high-ranking positions in *chaebol* bureaucracies. Building on this foundation, the Koreans themselves expanded their knowledge and social networks in China, enabling the *chaebol* to "ride the Chinese dragon" and benefit from its growth. This case highlights how the injection of diversity (i.e., knowledge of the Chinese context) in the form of Korean Chinese, and the acceptance of these individuals and their China-specific knowledge, helped the *chaebol* adapt to a difficult foreign market and thrive there for the better part of a decade.

Overall, the chapters in this volume highlight how Korea might overcome the constraints imposed by the legacy of a developmental state. Policy innovations undertaken by the state and strategy and operational innovations undertaken by SMEs and the *chaebol* have the potential to move Korea beyond the substantial challenges that is currently facing. Yet, these innovations cannot be implemented without building dynamic capabilities related to creativity and absorptive capacity. The core contention of this volume is that Korean society can build these capabilities, provided that it continues moving towards tolerating and even embracing the gender and national diversity increasingly found there. Maintaining and nurturing these social trends, then, takes on an instrumental economic importance beyond their considerable intrinsic value.

Notes

1 www.koreatimes.co.kr/www/news/biz/2016/03/123_199360.html.
2 www.koreatimes.co.kr/www/news/biz/2016/07/123_208379.html.
3 Platts. 2015. www.platts.com/news-feature/2015/metals/south-korea-steel-growth/index.
4 World Steel Association. 2014. "Top steel producing companies". www.worldsteel. org/statistics/top-producers.html.
5 http://blogs.platts.com/2016/05/02/regionality-china-steel-export-juggernaut/.
6 http://english.yonhapnews.co.kr/news/2015/02/25/60/0200000000AEN20150225002 000320F.html.
7 The Shipbuilders' Association of Japan, March 2016 Shipbuilding Statistics. www. sajn.or.jp/e/statistics/Shipbuilding_Statistics_Mar2016e.pdf.
8 www.koreatimes.co.kr/www/news/biz/2016/05/123_201454.html.
9 www.wsj.com/articles/iranian-oil-shipping-companies-strike-2-4-billion-south-korean-ship-deal-1465289444.
10 www.bloomberg.com/news/articles/2016-05-18/mass-layoffs-loom-in-south-korea-as-corporate-revamp-starts.
11 www.gartner.com/newsroom/id/3323017.
12 www.wsj.com/articles/samsung-profits-hurt-by-smartphone-price-declines-1438215502.
13 www.extremetech.com/computing/211972-htc-declared-effectively-worthless-lgs-profit-margins-fall-to-a-penny-a-phone.
14 www.bloomberg.com/news/articles/2015-06-25/china-has-big-plans-for-homegrown-chips.
15 Stephen Roach and Sharon Lam 2010, as quoted in www.mckinsey.com/global-themes/asia-pacific/south-korea-finding-its-place-on-the-world-stage.
16 *The Economist*. 2015.
17 Given its intermediate position between China and Japan and proximity to the USA, Korea had geographic advantages as a logistics hub, and the administration proposed that Incheon International Airport be promoted as an air freight transshipment center, that Gwangyang and Busan ports enhance their transshipment roles, and that the government should cooperate with North Korea, China, and Russia to rebuild rail linkages across Asia into Europe. See K. Lee (2004). This initiative was largely successful. Incheon International Airport has become one of the five busiest airports in the world in terms of air cargo, becoming one of the main hubs not only for Korean Air Cargo, but also for foreign firms like Polar Air Cargo, Air China Cargo, British Airways World Cargo, Cargolux, and China Airlines Cargo. Likewise, the Port of Busan experienced strong growth and became the second largest transshipment port in the world. See Airport-Technology.com. 2010. "The World's Top Ten Cargo Hub Airports." March 9, 2010, www.airport-technology.com/features/feature78850/; Ascutia, Romelda. 2013. "Korea, Malaysia ports achieve traffic growth in 2012." January 28, 2013, www.portcalls.com/korea-malaysia-ports-achieve-traffic-growth-in-2012/.
18 See K. Lee (2004); Presidential Transition Committee (2003).
19 H. Kim (2009).
20 http://blogs.wsj.com/korearealtime/2014/06/17/as-western-banks-retreat-japan-and-china-banks-profit-in-korea/; www.koreatimes.co.kr/www/news/biz/2016/04/488_20 1787.html; http://koreajoongangdaily.joins.com/news/article/Article.aspx?aid=3018603.
21 Mundy (2015).
22 Min (2016).
23 Hasung Jang, the former dean of Korea University Business School, as cited by Mundy (2015).
24 Mundy (2015); www.mckinsey.com/global-themes/asia-pacific/south-korea-finding-its-place-on-the-world-stage.

25 The OECD (2016a, 2016b) defines the life expectancy at birth and the total fertility rate as follows: "Life expectancy at birth is defined as how long, on average, a newborn can expect to live, if current death rates do not change."

The total fertility rate in a specific year is defined as the total number of children that would be born to each woman if she were to live to the end of her child-bearing years and give birth to children in alignment with the prevailing age-specific fertility rates. It is calculated by totaling the age-specific fertility rates as defined over five-year intervals. Assuming no net migration and unchanged mortality, a total fertility rate of 2.1 children per woman ensures a broadly stable population.

26 www.pewresearch.org/fact-tank/2014/02/04/the-countries-that-will-be-most-impacted-by-aging-population/.

27 www.economist.com/news/briefing/21601248-generation-old-people-about-change-global-economy-they-will-not-all-do-so; http://crr.bc.edu/wp-content/uploads/2013/05/wp_2013-111.pdf.

28 www.marketwatch.com/story/japan-consumer-prices-up-but-spending-sluggish-2015-12-24.

29 Hewitt (2002).

30 Chang (2008); Moon (2016).

31 Stinchcombe (1965); Marquis (2003).

32 Beckman, Haunschild, and Phillips (2004); Borgatti and Foster (2003).

33 After democratization, Roh Tae-woo shifted the role of the state away from authoritarian control to institutional regulation. The developmental state receded even further under Kim Young Sam's *segyehwa* agenda, when Korea adopted market mechanisms as a condition for joining the OECD and the WTO. The aftermath of the Asian Financial Crisis of 1997 represented a last hurrah of state-directed industrial policy, as corporate insolvencies triggered a flurry of statist intervention in the form of "big deals" or "workouts" to rescue insolvent firms that were "too big to fail." Yet, after Korea and the surviving *chaebol* emerged from the financial crisis, the state experienced IMF-mandated reductions in formal authority and coordinative capabilities. In particular, the policy banks were converted into market-oriented institutions, largely under foreign ownership. See Moon (2016), p. 39; E.M. Kim (1999); Thurbon (2016).

34 Barney (1991); Teece, Pisano, and Shuen (1997); see Moon (2016), pp. 100–102 for a review.

35 Moon (2016).

36 Mednick (1962).

37 Goffman (1974); Sewell (1992).

38 Steve Jobs, 2005 Commencement Address at Stanford University. http://news.stanford.edu/2005/06/14/jobs-061505/.

39 Jacobs (1969); Lucas (1988).

40 Zucker (1977).

41 Scott (2000).

42 Burt (1995); Granovetter (1973).

43 Coleman (1988); McDonald and Westphal (2003).

44 Fleming, Mingo, and Chen (2007); Perry-Smith (2006); Capaldo (2007); Cattani and Ferriani (2008).

45 Bian (1997); Xiao and Tsui (2007); Ma, Huang, and Shenkar (2011).

46 Granovetter (1973).

47 See Podolny and Page (1998) for a review.

48 Stinchcombe (1990).

49 Powell (1990).

50 Hofstede (1980); House et al. (1992).

51 Shin (2006).

52 Moon (2016), pp. 13–15; Eckert (2016), new book.
53 Moon (2016), p. 29.
54 Although the RBV focused on resources and capabilities directly controlled by firms, it acknowledged that many of the most important are embedded within society. Scholars as diverse as Porter (1990) and Saxenian (1996) highlight the importance of resources and capabilities embedded within society, ranging from the know-how that circulates through local social networks "as if it were in the air" Marshall (1920), to a localized labor pool that possesses important specialized skills.
55 2013 statistics from the OECD.
56 Statistics Korea data for June 2011.
57 www.koreatimes.co.kr/www/news/nation/2016/06/116_207878.html
58 www.newsweek.com/samsungs-female-executives-shatter-south-koreas-glass-ceiling-65613.
59 Shin (2006); Shin and Choi (2015).
60 World Values Survey Waves 5 and 6.
61 OECD (2014).

References

Barney, Jay. 1991. "Firm resources and sustained competitive advantage". Journal of Management 17: 99–120.

Beckman, Christine M., Pamela R. Haunschild, and Damon J. Phillips. 2004. "Friends or strangers? Firm-specific uncertainty, market uncertainty, and network partner selection." Organization Science 15(3): 259–275.

Bian, Y. 1997. Bringing strong ties back in: Indirect ties, network bridges, and job searches in China. American Sociological Review 62(3): 366–385.

Borgatti, Stephen P. and Pacey C. Foster. 2003. "The Network Paradigm in Organizational Research: A Review and Typology." Journal of Management 29: 991.

Burt, Ronald S. 1995. Structural Holes: The Social Structure of Competition. Cambridge: Harvard University Press.

Capaldo, Antonio. 2007. "Network structure and innovation: The leveraging of a dual network as a distinctive relational capability." Strategic Management Journal 28(6): 585–608.

Cattani, Gino, and Simone Ferriani. 2008. "A core/periphery perspective on individual creative performance: Social networks and cinematic achievements in the Hollywood film industry." Organization Science 19(6): 824–844.

Chang, Sea-Jin. 2008. Sony vs. Samsung: The Inside Story of the Electronics Giants' Battle for Global Supremacy. Wiley.

Choi, Byung-Sun. 1993. "Financial Policy and Big Business in Korea: The Perils of Financial Regulation." In The Politics of Finance in Developing Countries, ed. S. Haggard, C. H. Lee and S. Maxfield. Ithaca: Cornell University Press, 93–122.

Coleman, James S. 1988. "Social capital in the creation of human capital." American Journal of Sociology: S95–S120.

Eckert, Carter J. Park Chung Hee and Modern Korea: The Roots of Militarism, 1866-1945. Cambridge, MA: Harvard University Press.

Fleming, Lee, Santiago Mingo and David Chen. 2007. "Collaborative brokerage, generative creativity, and creative success". Administrative Science Quarterly 52(3): 443–475.

Goffman, Erving. 1974. Frame analysis: An essay on the organization of experience. Cambridge, MA: Harvard University Press.

Granovetter, Mark S. 1973. "The Strength of Weak Ties." American Journal of Sociology: 1360–1380.

Hewitt, Paul S. 2002. "Depopulation and Ageing in Europe and Japan: The Hazardous Transition to a Labor Shortage Economy." International Politics and Society.

Hofstede, G. 1980. Culture's Consequences: International Differences in Work-related Values. Newbury Park, CA: Sage Publications.

House, R., M. Javidan, P. Hanges and P. Dorfman. 2002. "Understanding cultures and implicit leadership theories across the globe: an introduction to project GLOBE." Journal of World Business 37: 3–10.

Howe, Neil, Richard Jackson and Keisuke Nakashima. 2007. The Aging of Korea: Demographics and Retirement Policy in the Land of the Morning Calm. Center for Strategic and International Studies.

Jacobs, Jane. 1969. The Economy of Cities. Random House.

Jung, K. 2015. "Change in the Export Competitiveness of China, Japan, and Korea." KDI report.

Kim, Eun Mee. 1999. "Crisis of the Developmental State in South Korea." Asian Perspective 23(2), 35–55.

Kim, Hansoo. 2009. "Seoul as an International Financial Centre: Roadmap, Progress and Challenges." In Competition among Financial Centres in Asia-Pacific: Prospects, Benefits, Risks and Policy Challenges. Eds. Soogil Young, Dosoung Choi, Jesus Seade and Sayuri Shirai. Singapore: ISEAS Publishing.

Lee, Kang-Kook. 2004. "Korea, Northeast Asian Economic Hub Country?: A Critical Study on the New Government Strategy." Ritsumeikan International Affairs 2, 1–25.

Lim, Suk-Jun. 1997. "Politics of Industrialization: Formation of Divergent Industrial Orders in Korea and Taiwan." Ph.D. dissertation, University of Chicago.

Lucas, Robert E. Jr. 1988. "On the Mechanics of Economic Development." Journal of Monetary Economics 22, 3–42.

Ma, R., Y. C. Huang and O. Shenkar. 2011. "Social networks and opportunity recognition: A cultural comparison between Taiwan and the United States." Strategic Management Journal 32(11): 1183–1205.

Marquis, Christopher. 2003. "The pressure of the past: Network imprinting in intercorporate communities." Administrative Science Quarterly 48(4): 655–689.

Marshall, Alfred. 1920. Principles of Economics: An Introductory Volume. London: MacMillan.

McDonald, Michael L., and James D. Westphal. 2003. "Getting by with the advice of their friends: CEOs' advice networks and firms' strategic responses to poor performance." Administrative Science Quarterly 48(1): 1–32.

Mednick, Sarnoff A. 1962. "The Associative Basis of the Creative Process." Psychological Review 69(3), 220–232.

Min, Catharina. 2016. "Korea Entrepreneurship Update: Trends and Dynamics." Presentation at the US-Asia Technology Program, Stanford University, April 26, 2016.

Moon, Hwy-chang. 2016. The Strategy for Korea's Economic Success. Oxford University Press.

Mundy, Simon. 2015. "South Korea aims for creative economy to end reliance on *chaebol*." Financial Times, June 24, 2015.

OECD. 2014. OECD Economic Surveys: Korea.

OECD. 2016a. "Labour Force Statistics by Sex and Age (Indicators)." Public-use data file and documentation. Accessed September 25, 2016. http://stats.oecd.org.

OECD. 2016b. "Fertility Rates (Indicator)." Public-use data file and documentation. Accessed September 3, 2016. https://dx.doi.org/10.1787/8272fb01-en.

Perry-Smith, Jill E. 2006. "Social yet creative: The role of social relationships in facilitating individual creativity." Academy of Management Journal 49(1): 85–101.

Podolny, Joel M., and Karen L. Page. 1998. "Network forms of organization." Annual Review of Sociology: 57–76.

Porter, M. E. 1990. The Competitive Advantage of Nations. New York: Free Press.

Powell, Walter W. 1990. "Neither Market Nor Hierarchy: Network Forms of Organization." Research in Organizational Behavior 12, 295–336.

Presidential Transition Committee. 2003. Conversation: White Paper of the 16th Presidential Transition Committee.

Saxenian, AnnaLee. 1994. Regional Advantage: Culture and Competition in Silicon Valley and Route 128. Cambridge: Harvard University Press.

Scott, W. Richard. 2000. Institutional change and healthcare organizations: From professional dominance to managed care. University of Chicago Press.

Sewell, William H. 1992. "A Theory of Structure: Duality, Agency, and Transformation." American Journal of Sociology 98(1): 1–29.

Shin Gi-Wook. 2006. Ethnic Nationalism in Korea: Genealogy, Politics, and Legacy. Stanford: Stanford Univ. Press.

Shin, Gi-Wook and Joon Nak Choi. 2015. Global talent: Skilled labor as social capital in Korea. Stanford University Press.

Stinchcombe, Arthur L. 1965. "Social Structure and Organizations." In Handbook of Organizations, ed. J. G. March. Chicago: Rand McNally & Co. pp. 142–193.

Stinchcombe, Arthur L. 1990. Information and Organizations. University of California Press.

Teece, David J., Gary Pisano, and Amy Shuen. 1997. "Dynamic capabilities and strategic management." Strategic Management Journal: 509–533.

The Economist. 2015. "A tiger in winter: A once fearsome economy struggles to fend off a deflationary funk." May 28, 2015.

Thurbon, Elizabeth. 2016. Developmental Mindset: The Revival of Financial Activism in South Korea. Cornell University Press.

Woo, Jung-en. 1991. Race to the Swift: State and Finance in Korean Industrialization. New York: Columbia University Press.

Xiao, Z., and A. S. Tsui. 2007. "When brokers may not work: The cultural contingency of social capital in Chinese high-tech firms." Administrative Science Quarterly 52(1): 1–31.

Zucker, Lynne G. 1977. "The role of institutionalization in cultural persistence". American Sociological Review: 726–743.

2 Corporate strategy and the competitiveness of Korean electronics firms versus their Japanese and Chinese counterparts

Hyung Oh Lee and Hyung-Deok Shin

Korean industrial firms (i.e., *chaebol*) have risen to global prominence in the past two decades. In many markets across the world, firms like LG and Samsung have become household names, often displacing Japanese competitors in prominence. Recent trends, however, have been far less favorable; as described in Chapter 1, the *chaebol* have been struggling to maintain market share in the face of increasingly sophisticated Chinese competition. Examining both of these phenomena, we analyze the competitiveness of Korean electronics firms against Japanese and Chinese competitors in this chapter.

We focus on corporate strategy because it seems to have a critical influence on competitive advantage, especially in increasingly globalized markets. Many comparative studies on national competitiveness among Korea, Japan, and China investigated trade imbalances, either in aggregate (Jung 2016) or in specific industry sectors (Kim 2010; Rui and Liu 2014; Son 2014). Such studies viewed trade imbalances as resulting from the aggregate behaviors of firms in each country. The drawback of this approach, however, is that aggregate statistics obscure the actual behaviors of individual firms—the real source of national competitiveness. Disaggregating the distinct corporate strategies of different firms, especially across different countries, has grown even more important given the globalization of business activities.

We chose the electronics industry to highlight the nexus between corporate strategy and globalization, within an industry where firms from the three countries have led the world market at least since the 1980s and where there have been changes in their relative competitiveness. Here, we select two representative firms from each country—Samsung Electronics Co., Ltd. (Samsung) and LG Electronics Co., Ltd. (LG) in Korea; Hitachi, Ltd. (Hitachi) and Panasonic Corporation (Panasonic) in Japan; and Huawei Technologies (Huawei) and Haier Electronics Group Co. Ltd. (Haier) in China—as cases of successful strategic adaptation in recent decades. We answer two questions raised in Chapter 1. The first is why Korean firms, especially Samsung, have been able to catch up to and even to surpass Japanese firms in competitiveness in the 2000s. The second is how Korean firms can sustain competitive advantage in the future in the face of severe competition against Japanese and Chinese firms. We answer these questions by proposing a framework for analyzing corporate strategies, and using this framework to examine changes in competitiveness among the three countries' electronics firms. We conclude this chapter by discussing the policy implications of our findings and suggesting topics for future study.

Analytical framework

There are two types of strategy for a firm—*corporate strategy*, which deals with entry into or exit from specific industries or geographic markets, and *competitive strategy*, which deals with how to compete effectively within these markets. This chapter focuses on corporate strategy, while Chapter 3 of this volume (Cho et al.) focuses on competitive strategy.

Corporate strategy has three elements: *vertical integration*, or whether to enter or exit a business vertically linked to the firm's current business lines; *diversification strategy*, or whether to enter or exit a business unrelated to the firm's current businesses; and *global strategy*, or which national markets to enter or exit. While the globalization of the firm might appear to be most salient to the global strategy aspect of this framework, it is also relevant to the other two.

We examined corporate strategies for two firms from each country that represent what we believe to be each country's best business models. In Korea, we selected Samsung and LG as representative electronics firms, which initially depended on the domestic market but are now global market leaders. In Japan, we selected Hitachi and Panasonic as the two largest firms by sales and gross profit in 2014. Although Sony remains one of the largest Japanese electronics firms, we did not select Sony because of its relatively low operating profit in recent years, making it unsuitable as a case of successful adaptation. While Hitachi and Panasonic also suffered low performance for many years, they recently recovered from their business slumps through strategic adaptation. In China, we selected Huawei and Haier because the former has grown to be a global leader in the telecommunication equipment industry and the latter has gained competitiveness in home appliances.

The performance of Korean, Japanese, and Chinese firms

To provide a baseline understanding of electronics firms in Korea, Japan, and China and their competitive dynamics, we begin by comparing their sales and operating profit. Our data were collected from public documents—Saeop Bogoseo (Business Report) for Korean firms, Yukashoken Hokokusyo (Market Securities Report) for Japanese firms, and the annual reports issued by Chinese firms.

Figure 2.1 reports sales for our six focal firms. Sales for Samsung, Huawei, and Haier continuously increased through the period in general, sales for the two Japanese firms stayed constant, and sales for LG fluctuated. While Samsung's sales growth was outstanding through 2013, sales peaked in 2013 and have been declining since then.

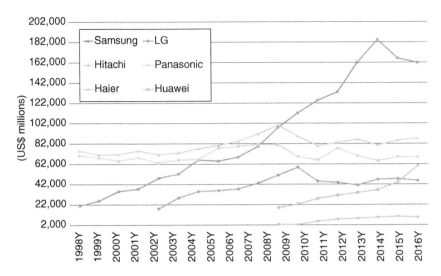

Figure 2.1 Comparison of total sales.

Figure 2.2 reports operating profits for our cases. While the broad trends in profits are quite similar to those for sales, there are several notable differences. The difference in operating profits is greater than the difference in sales between Samsung and its five rivals, indicating a consistently greater profit margin. Furthermore, operating profits for all firms fluctuate more than sales, especially for

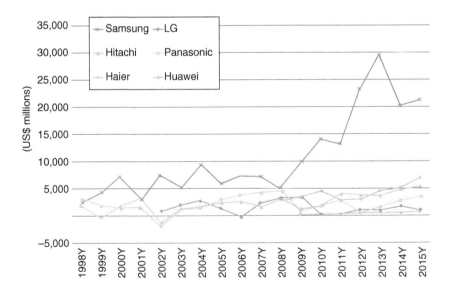

Figure 2.2 Comparisons of operating profit.

the Japanese firms. Finally, the operating profit of Huawei is more than that of the two Japanese firms in 2015. In the next section, we investigate the antecedents of these patterns.

Sources of the competitive advantage

One of our research questions is why Korean firms, especially Samsung, have gained competitive advantages against Japanese firms. We look for answers to this question from the perspective of corporate strategy, particularly its global and diversification aspects. Although the main focus of this section is to compare and contrast Korean and Japanese firms, we also include Chinese firms to provide a baseline for further discussion.

Global strategy

We examine the global strategy of Korean, Japanese, and Chinese firms by disaggregating sales by region. Ideally, we would examine not only the global distribution of sales but also production. However, data on the global distribution of production was not reported by our focal firms. In Figure 2.3, we can see that the domestic sales of Samsung have been stable through our study period but that foreign sales dramatically increased between 2005 and 2013. This increase accounts for much of Samsung's rapid growth. Foreign sales in 2013 were more than three times those in 2005, and growth continued through 2013. Sales in North America and Europe increased particularly rapidly since 2008; North American sales ended up being more than three times larger domestic sales. We can also see that this sales increase was achieved not only from North America

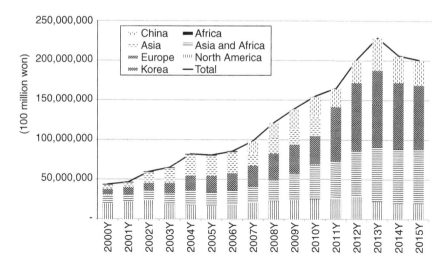

Figure 2.3 Samsung sales by region.

and Europe but also from Asia and Africa. However, foreign sales dropped in 2014, which led to the drop of total sales and operating profits as shown in Figures 2.1 and 2.2.

Foreign markets are just as important for LG. Figure 2.4 shows that the ratio of foreign sales to domestic sales is very high, a pattern similar to Samsung's. Although there have been some fluctuations, the foreign market growth of LG generally accelerated through 2014. North American sales have made up the largest proportion of the total, while the size of other foreign markets has remained relatively evenly distributed. The relatively small size of the Korean domestic market may have contributed to the high foreign market ratio of Samsung and LG.

The two Japanese firms have had relatively stable foreign sales over time compared with the two Korean firms. For the past decade, the ratio of foreign sales to total sales for both firms was consistently only around 50 percent. For Hitachi, sales to its largest foreign market (Asia excluding Japan) were consistently less than one-third of its sales to the domestic market. For Panasonic, the same ratio was less than one-quarter. In addition, sales from both developed and developing regions have been stable over the 1990s and 2000s. Taken together, these factors explain why the total sales of the Japanese firms did not fluctuate over time. We expect that other Japanese electronics firms would have experienced similar sales patterns.

As a further reference point, we examine global sales for Chinese firms. The financial statements of Haier did not disaggregate foreign sales from total sales,

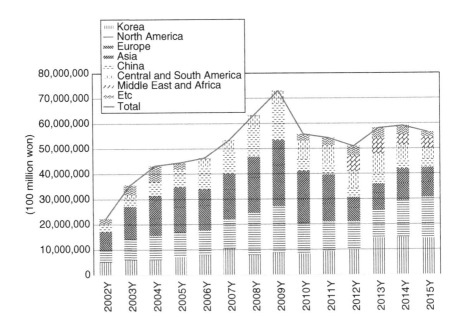

Figure 2.4 LG sales by region.

so we investigated only Huawei. Like Korean firms, Huawei depended highly on foreign markets for its growth. Although the proportion of domestic sales has increased recently, foreign sales were about twice domestic sales from 2010 to 2012, contributing to the growth of the firm (Figure 2.5).

Overall, Korean firms were successful because of their global market expansion. Although the relatively small size of the Korean domestic market might have helped motivate their overseas expansion, attempts by Korean firms to enter foreign markets also deserve credit. Simultaneously, the stagnation of total sales among Japanese firms in the 1990s and 2000s is related to the domestic market-oriented strategy of those firms. Indeed, Japan's relatively large domestic market may have contributed to stable business operation of Japanese firms, but it also discouraged them from pursuing for extensive foreign market exploration. In addition, Japanese firms tended to be satisfied with maintaining market share in developed countries, while Korean firms explored not only developed markets but also developing markets (Fujita 2013). Regarding Huawei, the firm not only used the huge Chinese domestic market but also pursued global expansion, and became a leader in the telecommunication equipment industry. It is now poised to also become a leader in other electronics products such as mobile phones.

Diversification strategy

Next, we move to the diversification strategy of Korean, Japanese, and Chinese firms. To analyze these firms' diversification strategies, we investigated the divisional sales composition of each firm. It was difficult to compare the diversification strategy of two different firms, as they placed the same products across different divisions. Furthermore, divisional placements often changed over time within a firm. Despite this limitation, the data nevertheless show the general outlines of the diversification strategy of each firm.

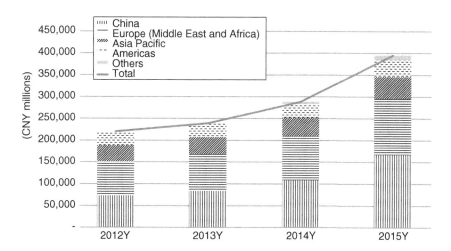

Figure 2.5 Huawei sales by region.

We begin by examining Samsung. Its major product groups include IT & Mobile Communications (IM), Consumer Electronics (CE), Semico (Semiconductor), and Display Panel (DP). Products in the IM and CE divisions are generally finished goods such as smartphones and TVs while products in the Semico and DP divisions are intermediate components such as memory chips and display panels. Samsung's sales growth has been led by the CE and IM divisions since 2008, implying that Samsung's rapid growth was enabled by its competence in producing finished goods such as smartphones and televisions, beyond its strong competitiveness in component businesses. However, sales from the IM and CE divisions decreased after 2013, when low-priced IM and CE products from China started to enter the global market. Meanwhile, Semico division sales increased and DP division sales did not decrease after 2013. It is worth noting that Samsung had a strong presence both in finished goods and intermediate components, and generated synergies across these lines in a process called "convergence" by Moon (2016). For instance, Samsung was able to leverage its know-how in semiconductor production in fabricating display panels, which used similar technologies and processes. In turn, Samsung's strengths across semiconductors and displays enabled it to become a market leader in mobile phones, for which semiconductors and displays were crucial components.

We find a similar pattern for LG, where sales growth was led by the Home Entertainment (HE), Mobile Communications (MC), and Home Appliance & Air Solution (H&A) divisions, which deal with finished goods such as the CE and IM divisions at Samsung. LG's sales come mainly from finished goods, unlike Samsung's mix of finished goods and parts. Note that HE division sales have been decreasing since 2013, when low-price Chinese competitors entered the global market. Sales from the Vehicle Components (VC) division first appeared in 2015.

Compared with these two Korean firms, the two Japanese firms focus more on products for industrial users. As these firms have had many divisions and changed their categorization schemes over time, it is not easy to understand changes in the business mix from sales by division. Thus, we compare business segment compositions as of 2005 and 2015 for them. We begin by examining Hitachi. While its business segment categorization is not the same across these two years, so that we cannot directly compare across them, the data nevertheless provide two insights. First, Digital Media & Consumer Products was an important business in 2005 (14.2 percent of total sales) but disappeared altogether by 2015 without replacement. Second, the Construction Machinery and Automotive Systems did not exist in 2005, but had grown to become important by 2015 (accounting for 17.6 percent of sales). This shows that Hitachi has recently focused more on industrial user businesses beyond its traditional focus on heavy electric businesses.

Panasonic has similarly changed its business orientation despite its traditional identity as a typical consumer electronics company in Japan. For the same reason as we did for Hitachi, we reviewed the business portfolios for two different years for Panasonic, 2011 versus 2015. We found that the importance of the consumer-oriented AVC Networks segments decreased significantly, declining from 24.8 percent of sales in 2011 to 15.0 percent only four years later. We also found that the importance of Automotive and Industrial Systems has increased significantly from 7.0 percent to 36.1 percent. This is important even after considering the addition of industrial systems to this category. We conclude that Panasonic has also shifted its focus toward industrial user products.

The opposite has been true for the two Chinese firms. From 2012 to 2015, Huawei grew very rapidly mainly in the network equipment business, and the proportion of sales produced by its Carrier Network Business remained high across all years. The proportion of sales generated by Huawei's Consumer Business, which includes mobile phones, has grown even more rapidly still, however, indicating that the company is gaining competitiveness not only in industrial business lines but also in consumer-oriented business lines. In contrast, Haier has focused more on consumer products. Its Integrated Channel Services Business includes its Distribution and Service Unit (TVs, refrigerators, air conditioners), E-Commerce Unit, and Logistics Unit. The Washing Machine Business and the Water Heater Business are also considered to be home appliance businesses. Overall, most of Haier's businesses lines are consumer-oriented. Indeed, the company recently acquired the home appliance division of General Electric and is now striving to be a global leader in home appliances.

These findings indicate that diversification strategy may have been the most important driver of Korean firms being able to catch up to their Japanese competitors. Korean firms have gained strong competitiveness particularly in finished products such as TV and mobile phones, while Japanese firms including Hitachi and Panasonic have shifted their focus away from consumer-oriented products in favor of industrial user products. Note that these two firms have epitomized successful transformation among Japanese industrial firms. Other Japanese firms such as Sanyo and Sharp have failed to transform and have disappeared as independent entities; Sanyo was wholly purchased by Panasonic in 2011 and Sharp was purchased by Taiwanese manufacturer Foxconn in 2016.

The success of Korean firms in the electronics industry can be explained by a changing business environment and firms' ability to adapt to this change. Recent studies (e.g., Moon 2016) suggested that the *chaebol* had capabilities that were well suited for benchmarking market leaders and leapfrogging them; this argument is addressed by the next chapter in this volume. These capabilities became particularly valuable given a change in the business environment towards digitalization and its effect on product architecture. We follow a perspective on product architecture that was originally proposed by Ulrich (1995) and later applied to the analysis of national competitiveness (e.g., Fujimoto 2006), which distinguishes between two types of product architectures, modular and integral. Modular architecture involves a one-to-one correspondence between functional and structural elements of a product, as in the case of personal computers. In contrast, integral architecture involves complex interdependencies between product functions and structures as in the case of automobiles (Fujimoto 2006). Digitalization changed the product architecture of many electronics products from integral to modular. Analog products such as the Walkman had an integral architecture needed to be built with precise coordination and combination of components. This architecture advantaged Japanese firms, as they were able to use their highly skilled employees (Fujita 2013). With the introduction of digital technology, however, the dominant product architecture became modular, as digital components became standardized. Products could now be assembled simply in modular fashion without having to carefully integrate the components. In the era of modular architecture, speed and investment timing became more important than highly skilled employees. Korean firms were good at speedy and intensive investment in digitalized products such as digital TV and mobile phones and eventually became the world leader in those industries. This explanation can be applied not only towards finished goods such as TV and mobile phones but also for components such as DRAM and LCD/LED panels, although their architecture is less modular than that of finished products.

A similar logic may be applicable to the recent success of Chinese competitors versus Korean firms. As seen in Figures 2.1, 2.3, and 2.4, sales for Korean firms have recently declined. The slump experienced by Samsung and LG in finished consumer goods may be attributable to the emergence of Chinese firms. We discuss this in greater detail below.

Vertical integration strategy

The crucial decision relating to vertical integration is whether to conduct an activity inside a firm or outsource it to other firms. In general, Japanese and Korean firms are similar in this respect, both featuring high levels of vertical integration perhaps because Korean firms learned not only technology but also management styles from Japanese firms. This strategy is called the one-set orientation, where a company attempts to internalize all activities relating to a product as much as possible. In addition, both Japanese and Korean firms have used long-term relationships with key suppliers, contingent on the growth rate of their businesses. Consequently, it is not easy to attribute the performance gap between Korean and Japanese firms to vertical integration.

It is worth noting that the high reliance on internal manufacturing of Korean and Japanese firms can be compared against the outsourcing practices of European and US firms. Western firms such as Philips and HP also internalized manufacturing in the past, but have shifted towards outsourcing since the 1980s. The strategic change was made possible by the rise of EMS (Electronics Manufacturing Service) firms such as Foxconn and Flextronics. Whether Korean and Japanese firms will change their vertical integration strategy and use EMS firms will become an important strategic issue for them in the future.

Although data on the vertical integration of Korean firms were limited, we imputed their degree of vertical integration by calculating the ratio of intermediate component purchases to total sales. When this ratio is low, the degree of vertical integration is high, which means the firm adds value internally. By this measure, Samsung is more vertically integrated than LG, and is becoming all the more vertically integrated; its ratio declined from 61.5 in 2009 to 36.9 in 2015. In contrast, LG is moving in the opposite direction, with its ratio increasing from 54.5 in 2012 to 58.3 in 2015. There are both advantages and disadvantages to vertical integration. On one hand, high vertical integration enables firms to capture a large proportion of the value from the products that they sell. Firms can also reduce the risks associated with their technological development by performing R&D internally. On the other hand, if many parts for finished goods are technologically standardized and modularized, too much dependence on vertical integration would expose a firm to the loss of competitiveness. If low-cost components became available in the market, less vertically integrated firms could easily shift their supply chains towards these components, while more vertically integrated firms could not easily make such a shift because they would have to abandon their own component production lines. Indeed, this may very well be one of the reasons why the foreign market sales of Samsung and LG dropped after 2013, which led to sales and operating profit declines.

Strategic issues for Korean firms in the future

As Figures 2.2 and 2.3 indicate, Korean firms have recently experienced performance declines since 2013. While there may be many reasons for these performance declines, two reasons seem to be particularly noteworthy—the rise of Chinese firms and the recovery of Japanese Firms. Chinese firms are gaining competitiveness rapidly in businesses such as air conditioners, TVs, and mobile phones in which Korean firms only recently were strong competitors. Simultaneously, Japanese firms have found a path for growth that avoids direct competition against Korean and Chinese firms. Today, the critical task for Korean firms is to sustain competitiveness and survive in the future. We will discuss this task by examining the three aspects of corporate strategy.

Global strategy

The rapid growth of Korean firms in the electronics industry was made possible by aggressive globalization across activities such as marketing and production. We classify the globalization processes of Korean firms into three stages. In the first stage (1980s and 1990s), Korean firms globalized mainly their sales and marketing activity and became export-oriented companies. In the second stage (after the 1997 financial crisis), they globalized not only sales and marketing but also their production. Korean firms are just about to enter a third stage, where an even wider range of activities including research and development and human resources management are being relocated to regions where they could be optimally performed, approaching what have become known as transnational organizations (Bartlett and Goshal 1989).

Although public statements do not show the global distribution of production for Korean firms, other data sources indicate that they were successful not only in globalizing their sales and marketing but also their production. As we noted earlier, the proportion of domestic sales for Samsung is only about 10 percent, while that of Hitachi and Panasonic is almost 50 percent. Furthermore, Samsung has intensively relocated production activities overseas to optimize their global production. For example, the production of mobile phones was done mainly in Gumi, Korea in the early 2000s but had been relocated to China by the late 2000s. Recently, however, as China has become increasingly expensive, Samsung has relocated about half of its total production to Vietnam. Note that Korean firms started by relocating the simple assembly of most finished products (i.e., TVs, notebook computers, mobile phones, etc.) to low-cost countries such as China, Vietnam, and Brazil, but continue to manufacture complex or sophisticated products such as DRAM memory chips and LCD panels in Korea.

A further issue is how much to globalize research and development and human resource management. To date, the *chaebol* have conducted most research and development in Korea, while the majority of top headquarters and subsidiary managers have been Korean. We expect that Korean firms will continue globalizing by spreading their research and development activities around the world, and also by hiring non-Korean senior managers.

Diversification strategy

Korean electronics firms have followed a successful diversification strategy, growing rapidly by winning market share away from Japanese firms in businesses such as TVs, refrigerators, semiconductors, LCD/LED panels, and others where Japanese and other developed country firms were market leaders. As mentioned earlier, the digitalization of technology and the resulting shift from integral to modular production had a major impact on the rising competitiveness of Korean firms. Also, the excellence of Korean firms at making intensive investments and rapidly conducting research and development, compared against the reluctance of Japanese firms to make timely investments, reinforced this trend.

The problem for Korean firms is that a similar change in competitiveness is about to happen, with Chinese firms unseating Korean market leaders. Chinese firms already have strong competitiveness in products featuring modular architecture (e.g., PCs and DVD players), with Chinese firms such as Lenovo already leading the global market. Now, Chinese firms are entering more sophisticated products such as mobile phones and are threatening the market position of Korean firms. We have already seen the early result of this change, as Samsung sales have began to drop while sales for Chinese firms such as Huawei in the mobile phone business and Haier in the TV business have increased. Similar patterns may someday materialize even in the semiconductor industry, where Korean firms are entrenched in a dominant market position (see Chapter 1).

How can Korean firms continue to compete in the future? We suggest that they leverage their speed advantage in products featuring modular architecture, as shown in Figure 2.6.

Fujimoto (2006) asserts that each country has competitiveness in a particular architecture, with Japanese firms having strong competitiveness in integral

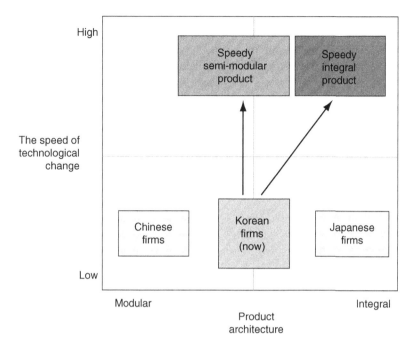

Figure 2.6 Future directions for Korean firms' diversification strategy.

architecture products, Chinese firms in labor-intensive modular architecture products, and Korean firms in capital-intensive modular architecture products. Based on this framework, we can roughly match the firms of each country with their current competitive advantages in this figure: Chinese firms for modular products, Korean firms for semi-modular products that combine the characteristics of both modular and integral products, and Japanese firms for integral products. The reason why Korean firms can be strong in semi-modular products is that their management style shares similarities with those of both Japanese and Chinese firms. Indeed, in many industries, high-tech materials and sophisticated parts are produced in Japan, intermediate products using Japanese materials and parts are produced in Korea, and then assembled into the final product in China. In this framework, Korean firms are now facing competition from Chinese firms as they are entering the semi-modular product area where Korean firms have been competitive.

There are two ways of strategically reacting to competition from Chinese firms. The first is to move toward integral product areas as Japanese firms such as Hitachi and Panasonic have focused more on industrial user products. Just moving toward integral products, however, may not be enough as Japanese firms have already established strong market positions there. Thus, we need to account for another dimension, the speed of technological change, where both the refined coordination of activities and speedy decision-making and execution are critical for success. Such business areas include the "Internet of Things" (IoT), biotechnology, healthcare-related equipment, automotive parts, and new materials. There, Korean firms may be able to use their corporate culture of speedy decision and investment (described in detail in Chapter 3 of this volume), something that their Japanese competitors currently lack. A second approach is to stay in semi-modular product lines such as mobile phone and to compete directly against Chinese firms. As Chinese firms have cost advantages, simply maintaining Korean firms' current positioning may not be enough. The dimension of speed can also be added here, and thus Korean firms need to explore products where speed is critical for competitive advantage. Particularly in these speedy semi-modular products, cost may be an important competitiveness factor, so that Korean firms need to explore production and research and development in low-cost countries.

Vertical integration strategy

As we mentioned earlier, Korean and Japanese firms both rely on high vertical integration. In contrast, Chinese firms seem less dependent on vertical integration. For example, Xiaomi is known for its aggressive outsourcing strategy, leaving only product development and marketing inside the company. We have less information on the vertical information strategies followed by Huawei and Haier, but Chinese firms seem to be more open to outsourcing than Korean and Japanese firms in general. The adoption of an open ecosystem for modular products may be the reason why we can find many successful start-ups in China and why some like Xiaomi have grown to become global firms in a short time; for more details, see Chapter 5 in this volume (Hsieh), which compares and contrasts the closed ecosystem found in Korea versus the more open ecosystem found in Taiwan.

It is difficult to evaluate the effectiveness of vertical integration or outsourcing as the decision is path-dependent. As is well known among mobile phone industry observers, Samsung has had a vertical integration-oriented strategy while Apple has had an outsourcing-oriented strategy—and both have been extremely successful. Yet, we suggest that Korean firms need to better use outsourcing and open innovation. Under an environment of rapid technological change, a firm cannot develop all the technology that it requires internally, and thus will need to leverage outsourcing and high-tech ventures. If Korean firms move more toward outsourcing and open innovation, this will have the further benefit of increasing business opportunities for SMEs and start-ups, discussed in more detail in Chapters 4 and 5 of this volume.

Conclusion and policy implications

The purpose of this chapter was to analyze the competitiveness of Korean firms against Japanese and Chinese firms focusing on the strategies of electronics firms. Based on the analysis of six firms across the three countries—Samsung and LG in Korea, Hitachi and Panasonic in Japan, and Huawei and Haier in China—we raised two research questions. The first question was why Korean firms, particularly Samsung, have been able to catch up to and surpass Japanese firms in the 2000s, and the second question was how Korean firms can sustain competitiveness in the future under competition from Japanese and Chinese firms.

We answered the first question by examining three aspects of corporate strategy. In global strategy, Korean firms were successful in expanding their businesses not only into developed countries but also into developing countries, while Japanese firms tended to rely highly on their large domestic market. In diversification strategy, the digitalization of technology in the electronics industry changed the dominant product architecture from integral to modular, and Korean firms succeeded in adapting to this environmental change. Korean firms gained competitiveness with speedy development and intensive investment in products such as TVs, mobile phones, and semiconductors, most of which were commercialized already by Japanese firms. Given the environmental change and the effective Korean strategic response to this change, some Japanese firms lost competitiveness and disappeared or otherwise weakened, while others like Hitachi and Panasonic retained their sales volume by focusing more on integral products for industrial customers. Finally, in vertical integration strategy, both Korean and Japanese firms relied on a high level of vertical integration, and we could not find a critical difference with regards to this aspect.

We also answered the second question by once again examining the three aspects of corporate strategy, but with a forward-looking focus. In global strategy, we expect that Korean firms would continue to globalize production activity not only for the relatively simple assembly of products such as TVs and notebook computers but also for more sophisticated tasks such as producing semiconductors. We also expect that Korean firms would globalize even their research and development and human resource management activities and eventually become truly transnational organizations. In diversification strategy, we found that the entry of Chinese firms into markets where Korean firms had competitive advantages was one of the reasons for the staggering losses experienced recently by some Korean firms. Also, we suggested that Korean firms needed to change their product portfolios either toward speedy integral products or toward speedy semi-modular products for sustaining competitiveness. Finally, in vertical integration, we discussed how Korean and Japanese firms were dependent on a relatively high level of vertical integration while Chinese firms were using outsourcing more actively. Considering this, we recommended that Korean firms ought to better use outsourcing and open innovation.

Although this chapter focused on corporate strategy, we also found implications for government policy. The goal of a multinational firm may not be closely related to that of the government of its origin, so that government policy needs to focus on how to stimulate firms to invest and to enhance employment inside the country regardless of their nationality. Based on this insight, we found several implications for the Korean government. First, the Korean government needs to think of policies which may enhance not only manufacturing industries but also high value-added service industries. As we have seen in the cases of Samsung and LG, they will further globalize production activities in the future, going beyond the overseas production of relatively simple modular products. Considering this, the government needs to provide Korean and foreign multi-national firms with incentives of keeping at least the production of sophisticated integral products and research and development activities for products manufactured overseas. The key issue is not to oppose the exodus of manufacturing from Korea but to retain and grow high value-added activities for firms by enhancing the location advantage of Korea with provision of refined government services to them. This is especially important as Korea has largely failed to attract high-value service industries such as finance (see Chapter 1).

Second, as Korea is no longer a suitable place for the production of simple modular products, the government needs to incentivize firms to focus more on research-intensive products or businesses. Korea needs to have location advantages eventually for highly sophisticated integral products or businesses, suggesting that the major industries of the country need to be restructured. To date, industries such as home appliances, automobiles, shipbuilding, commodity chemicals, and others were considered to be Korea's main industries. Yet, Korea will have difficulty in sustaining competitiveness in such industries, as Chapter 1 described. Restructuring Korea's industrial base has become a critical task.

Finally, the Korean government needs to reconsider the appropriate structure and scope of vertical integration for an industry. Up to this time, a pyramid structure with a *chaebol* affiliate at the top was considered to be inescapable in assembly-based industries such as automobile and electronics industries. The *chaebol* affiliate would be the spoke of the wheel, and its suppliers would radiate outwards. Indeed, cooperative coordination between a large firm and its suppliers has been emphasized in much government policy (see Chapter 5 for more details). This structure may still be effective in industries dealing with integral products where coordination is important. Given rapidly changing technology, however, a more egalitarian network structure may be more effective than a pyramid structure (see Chapters 1 and 5 in this volume). The government needs to incentivize firms to outsource and use open innovation more widely, particularly in speedy semi-modular products.

This chapter bases its findings and their implications on a small number of case studies, and further research needs to be done to overcome this limitation. Further investigation is needed regarding the detailed strategies of each firm to ensure internal validity. In addition, our analysis needs to be expanded to encompass a greater number of firms to ensure external validity, by making sure that our findings are consistent across this larger sample. Furthermore, the study needs to be expanded to include other industries to find more meaningful policy implications for improving Korean national competitiveness.

References

Bartlett, T. and S. Ghoshal. 1989. Managing Across Borders: The Transnational Solution. Harvard Business School Press.

Fujimoto, T. 2006. "Architecture-based Comparative Advantage in Japan and Asia." University of Tokyo, MMRC Discussion Paper, MMRC-F-94.

Fujita, T. 2013. "For the Revival of the Japanese Electronics Industry." JRI Review 6(7): 57–81.

Haier Electronics Group Co., Ltd., Annual Report.

Hitachi, Ltd., Yukasyoken-Hokokusyo (Marketable Securities Report).

Huawei Technologies Co., Ltd., Annual Report.

Jung, K. 2016. "Change in the Export Competitiveness of China, Japan, and Korea." KDI report.

Kim, K. 2010. "An Analysis of the Competitiveness of Korea's Domestic Car Component Industry with those of China and Japan." Journal of Global Business and Trade 6(2): 49–65.

LG Electronics Co., Ltd., Saeop-Bogoseo (Business Report).

Moon, Hwy-chang. 2016. The Strategy for Korea's Economic Success. Oxford University Press.

Panasonic Corporation, Yukasyoken-Hokokusyo (Marketable Securities Report).

Rui, L. and Z. Liu. 2014. "Comparative Research of Competitiveness and Influence Factors of Computer and Information Service Trade of South Korea, China and Japan." Journal of the Korea Society of Computer and Information, 19(12): 329–338.

Samsung Electronics Co., Ltd., Saeop-Bogoseo (Business Report).

Son, M. 2014. "A Comparative Analysis on the Competitiveness of the Korean, Chinese and Japanese Fashion Industries." Journal of Fashion Business, 18(6): 67–85.

Ulrich, K. 1995. "The Role of Product Architecture in the Manufacturing Firm." Research Policy, 24: 419–440.

3 Competitive strategy and the challenges for the *chaebol*

Myeong Hyeon Cho, Jonghoon Bae, Jaiho Chung, Sungchoon Kang, and Daesoo Kim

The rise of the *chaebol*—the industrial firms that dominate the Korean economy—has been nothing short of spectacular. The *chaebol* took leading positions in the global market for ships, automobiles, electronics, and many other industrial and consumer goods. Although the decision to enter these industries (i.e., corporate strategy, see Chapter 2 of this volume) contributed to this successful outcome, how the *chaebol* chose to compete in these industries (i.e., competitive strategy) has also mattered greatly. The so-called fast-follower strategy employed by the *chaebol*—rapidly imitating innovations and technological advances adopted by market leaders and leveraging cost advantages, attention to quality, and superior agility enabled the *chaebol* to leapfrog market incumbents (see Chapters 1 and 2 of this volume for details). In recent years, however, *chaebol* reliance on this competitive strategy has backfired, and the *chaebol* have lost market share in important overseas markets (see Chapters 1 and 2). In this chapter, we examine how the competitive strategy and operational attributes of Korean firms have helped achieve their dramatic rise through the 2000s, but have hindered the *chaebol* from adapting to a new competitive landscape during the past decade. We identify not only the factors that have historically contributed to the success of the *chaebol*, but also the challenges that Korean firms are facing in a struggle to transform themselves to become more competitive. We focus on three inter-related aspects of the way *chaebol* compete within specific industries: *competitive strategies*, *organizational structures* and *cultures*, and *operations*.

Competitive strategy

The previous chapter of this volume highlighted exports of consumer goods as the linchpin for *chaebol* success, at least for Samsung Electronics and LG. This corporate strategy was enabled by a fast-follower competitive strategy that enabled the *chaebol* to catch up and often surpass industry incumbents (Lee 2013). One element of this strategy, introduced in Chapter 1 of this volume, was aggressive investment into large-scale production to generate scale economies, backed by government-sponsored capital injections. Such investments were most effective in combination with quick decision-making and execution (Holstein and Nakarmi 1995), as timely execution of a fast-follower strategy is critical. In Korea, this combination enabled Korean firms to expedite preemptive investments in well-defined markets at scale (e.g., Moon 2016). Korean practitioners continue to believe that quickness, flexibility, and versatility are critical to survival and growth in fierce global competition. In this *palli palli* (i.e., quickly, quickly) business culture, top management constantly pushes for new product development and introduction to shorten time to market (Blasi and Puig 2002; Bae 1997). This belief has been institutionalized into a quick and responsive management style and rapid technology adoption (Bae and Lawler 2000; Kirk 2001; Lau et al. 2005).

The combination of aggressive capital investments and rapid decision-making and execution was especially effective where fast-changing production technologies rendered the competitive advantage of incumbents temporary. In particular, a shorter product life cycle as well as the arrival of new product and process innovations reset the clock for new entrants, reducing the barriers to entry posed by the incumbents' technological leadership. The semiconductor industry highlights this effect. Advances in miniaturization required the invention of new processes and the purchase of new tools for new generations of memory chips, eroding the advantages of incumbency over time.

This strategy has faltered in recent years, as low-cost Chinese competitors have stripped away the *chaebol*'s cost competitiveness. As examined in Chapter 1 of this volume, Chinese firms not only have a large, captive domestic market but also access to even greater financial resources than the *chaebol*, giving them the potential to reach even greater scale economies. The standard strategic response to this challenge would be to differentiate one's products from Chinese goods. Yet, the *chaebol* have had difficulty with this approach. Quality competitiveness has not proven to differentiate the *chaebol* enough from global competitors, and further differentiation remains difficult as long as the *chaebol* are pursuing a fast-follower strategy that remains imitative at its core. While some observers (e.g., Moon 2016) have argued that the *chaebol* have been more innovative than commonly believed, especially at incrementally improving existing products, there is a broad consensus that the *chaebol* have proven ineffective at generating the kinds of disruptive innovations that can create new markets while obsoleting existing ones.

The current technology landscape has also presented a fundamental challenge to the fast-follower strategy. Information technology has emerged as a so-called general purpose technology with an uncertain impact on business practices and consumer behaviors. For instance, "big data" and machine learning represent important trends with unpredictable outcomes. Additionally, digitalization and large-scale custom production alleviates time compression diseconomies and lowers entry barriers, further eroding *chaebol*s' advantages versus Chinese competitors. As discussed in Chapters 1 and 2, the *chaebol* have lost much market share to these newly sophisticated competitors.

Although the *chaebol* have largely recognized these challenges, they have found it difficult to switch away from the fast-follower strategy towards true market leadership. Practitioners have testified that pioneering and adapting to international markets has been a challenge (Shin et al. 2015), as the *chaebol* have developed an organizational structure and operational processes that remain tightly aligned with the fast-follower strategy. We discuss these impediments to strategic change in the following sections.

Founder-centric organizational structures

Leadership by founders and their families played an important role in the past success of the *chaebol*, but has become less beneficial. The strong control rights that accrue to the founders and their families has made possible a redeployment of large-scale capital investments from one project to another even when the equity market is skeptical about their prospects. Such rapid and decisive decision-making has proven crucial for the success of the fast-follower strategy (see Moon 2016 for case studies). At the same time, this process has not proven conducive to making commitments to uncertain markets that have yet to become well-defined, especially those involving emerging technologies. Although the fast-follower strategy has required firms to migrate swiftly to adopt technological advances within a predictable field, such as migrating towards increasingly miniaturized architectures within semiconductors, it has had little to do with discovering novel opportunities. Consequently, the *chaebol* have had little experience pioneering markets for new products, although they have certainly become expert at moving into markets for established ones.

Furthermore, the founders' focus on control right over their companies leave little room for developing capabilities for merging or partnering with external actors. The fear of losing managerial control causes founders and their families to develop a conservative attitude towards new organizational forms, fearing that change may disrupt control rights over the firm. As a result, M&A activities are infrequent in Korea not because the financial institutions do not provide adequate support services, but because the founders prefer in-house development by maintaining equity control over their companies. For this reason, a typical M&A in Korea involves bank-led corporate restructuring where creditors (i.e., banks) take over control rights from the founders or current management and search for M&A partners themselves. In other words, only troubled companies with non-performing loans become targets for M&As, so that healthy firms never develop M&A capabilities.

A closely related problem is that the inward-looking tendency of the *chaebol* makes strategic alliances and other forms of partnership difficult to envision or execute. In addition to the organizational conservatism of senior managers, the vertical integration of many *chaebol* (see Chapter 2) prevents a search for strategic partners to co-invest resources into expensive, long-term projects (Chang and Hong 2000). Accordingly, the *chaebol* broadly lack the ability to cooperate with external partners. Along with insufficient experience with M&As, difficulties forming alliances imposes difficulty evaluating emerging technologies and long-term strategies, as the *chaebol* cannot leverage external parties more knowledgeable about such technologies and strategies. For example, the management at SK Telecom failed to recognize the market potential of free data services such as KakaoTalk, a Korean equivalent of WhatsApp, based on their orientation towards capital-intensive access lines. For these reasons, the *chaebol* have largely been locked out of emerging platform businesses where the creation of new value comes from horizontal coordination with external partners.

These problems manifest themselves in the way the *chaebol* leverage supply chains. Competition no longer occurs between rival firms, but rather, between rival supply chains. Thus, the competitiveness of supply chains, which produce goods and services via intra-firm and inter-firm coordination, matters greatly.[1] The potential gains from improved supply chain management go beyond production efficiency and quality improvements. Effective supply chain management can leverage the ability of suppliers to innovate, contingent on systemic linkages across firms based on inter-firm trust and information exchanges, and the sharing of value in an open innovation network. Using innovative intermediate components would substantially enhance the competitiveness of the end product—a concept that *chaebol* such as Samsung understand well (see Moon 2016).[2] Yet, the *chaebol* fall painfully short of best practices in supply chain management (Handfield et al. 2009). In Korea, the supply chain is still not considered a driver of shareholder value and competitive differentiation, and supply chain strategies are not well incorporated into business strategy planning. For this reason, the supply chain planning process has not been sufficiently adaptive, and the *chaebol* have been reluctant to expand beyond first-tier suppliers in terms of outsourcing and strategic alliances. Changing this state of affairs will require both operational and management and information system changes. Operationally, what is needed is for the *chaebol* to move beyond hierarchical organizational structures and decision-making at the divisional level towards a hybrid between centralized planning and control and decentralized operations and execution, giving lower level managers the opportunity to propose cooperative ventures. This hybrid model can be held together with integrated information technology systems.[3] In general, supply network integration and collaboration needs to be enhanced through information sharing, transparency, and visibility among internal functions and with strategic suppliers. This phenomenon also highlights how *chaebol* founders' obsession with control rights hinders the possibility that small and medium-sized companies might benefit from the spillovers of knowledge or access key resources at a negotiable price, directly resulting in the inability of the small and mid-sized firms to scale up early yet fast-growing business opportunities (see Chapter 4).

Organizational culture and human resource management

Beyond an aversion to uncertainty and the inability to work with external parties, the founder-centric organization of the *chaebol* also tends to make the firm excessively reliant on informal culture and interpersonal ties. The *chaebol* typically feature low standardization and high centralization. Given the diversified nature of many *chaebol* across many different, vertically integrated industries, standardization tends to be difficult across business units. Instead of relying on internal processes that remain poorly defined and undocumented, cooperation across business units tends to rely on the individual capabilities and interpersonal relationships of generalist workers. In turn, this tendency tends to preclude attempts to formalize the internal workings of the company, and makes it necessary to centralize to maintain the firm's cohesion. For these reasons, the general trading company, a template that goes back to the colonial era and prevailed in the corporate worlds of Japan and Korea after the 1950s, remains a widely accepted model of organization in Korea (Kim 1986; Sarathy 1985). For example, the *chaebol* initially followed an export-oriented growth strategy based around a general trading company that sourced input factors globally. In these entities, formal process controls were virtually absent and a small group—often a single employee—was responsible for the entire business development process. The *chaebol* imprinted these work practices across their subsidiaries over time.

A few leading *chaebol* have recently taken steps to reform their control systems. One template has been General Electric (GE), well known for having a process-oriented work system coordinated centrally by the general office and motivated by competitive compensation schemes. Samsung has adapted GE-like organizational processes to a founder-dominated governance structure (Song and Lee 2014; Chang 2008). Similarly, SK Telecom adopted a CIC (company-in-company) structure in 2007 (Lee and Bae 2011) where it delegated control over diversified product lines to four autonomous product divisions, whose operations were reviewed and coordinated by the general office under the control of CEO. However, other *chaebol* have largely retained their orientation towards informality.

The driving forces behind the *chaebol*'s rapid growth have been attributed not only to the unique structures and management systems of Korean firms, but also to highly skilled and committed Korean employees. During the early period of economic growth, with a GDP growth rate of around 8 percent per year from 1970 to 1997, the external labor market was not well developed. Building on a Confucian tradition that highlighted employee-employer interdependence (i.e., paternalistic employment relationships), the *chaebol* relied heavily on internal labor markets (ILMs), where internal employees were trained and maintained, being shielded from the competition exerted by external labor markets. In this context, Korean firms have maintained internal staffing, seniority-based rewards and promotions, and lifetime employment to sustain employee commitment and loyalty. Because ILMs basically encouraged employers to stabilize employment and discourage employees from leaving the organization, they also engendered rigid administrative rules and customs largely based on past practices and experiences. Consequently, ILMs helped the *chaebol* develop firm-specific skills, improve employee commitment, and facilitate homogeneity and solidarity in the work group, which helped the *chaebol* decisively execute on emerging opportunities, supporting and enabling the fast-follower strategy.

Since the early 1990s, globalization and the gradual decline in the growth rate of the Korean economy have raised questions about the advisability of continuing this distinctive Korean employment system (Whitley 1999). Intensified international competition has increased the need for the *chaebol* to improve competitiveness by cutting labor costs. The growing mobility of capital and advances in information technology have resulted in Korean firms receiving more exposure to global (especially US-based) firms' employment practices (Kim and Kim 2003). In response to this change in the economic environment, some Korean firms turned to US-style employment practices to achieve greater numerical and external flexibility. However, US-style performance-oriented employment practices leading to more internal competition among employees were initially regarded as too radical by *chaebol* employees, who were strongly committed to cultural norms of collectivism and were accustomed to lifetime employment and reward stability. Thus, US-style employment practices were not widely accepted by Korean firms.

Radical changes in the Korean employment systems did not take place until Korea experienced an unexpected financial crisis in November 1997. In 1998, the Korean GDP shrank by 5.8 percent, the unemployment rate increased from around 2 percent to 6.8 percent, and many large firms went bankrupt, were liquidated, or merged. With this crisis, Korean firms began to be criticized for their traditional structures and management systems such as reckless expansion, high financial leverage, feudal governance structures, and paternalistic employment relationships. In particular, the involvement of the International Monetary Fund (IMF), through which the US insisted on spreading an Anglo American market-driven system to other economies, pushed Korean firms to adopt the US-style employment model as a national standard. Although some Korean firms had begun to change their employment practices during the rapid globalization of the early 1990s, the East Asian financial crisis provided critical momentum for dramatic institutional changes in Korean employment practices toward the US-style model (Alakent and Lee 2010). In fact, data from several surveys by the Korean Ministry of Labor of about 5,000 firms with 100 or more employees show that the proportion of firms that adopted performance-related pay rapidly increased from 3.6 percent in 1997 to 12.7 percent in 1998, to 23 percent in 2000, and to 41.9 percent in 2001 (Kang and Yanadori 2011). Since 2000 Korean firms have actively imitated employment practices (e.g., forced ranking like GE's vitality curve) of successful global firms to improve flexibility and performance.

Through this evolution, Korean firms have developed a unique HRM system that mixes a traditional ILM and a performance-oriented market system. Most Korean firms now fill a number of vacancies by hiring experienced workers from the outside, but still hire many entry-level college graduates through annual open recruitment into an ILM. Korean firms also guarantee employment security for regular employees and simultaneously seek employment flexibility through the use of temporary workers and outsourcing. Employee pay and rewards are determined on the forced ranking system, which identifies a company's best and worst performing employees, using person-to-person comparisons. Hierarchical structure and centralized coordination are used to coordinate and control individuals' effort and intra-firm activities. These employment practices have enforced work values emphasizing a hard-working culture, hierarchical control, and a short-term performance orientation in Korean firms, which have supported the successful implementation of the fast-follower strategy of Korean firms. More specifically, as organizational members with employment security interacted with one another over a long period of time, they could build trust with one another, which decreased their motives for opportunistic behaviors and increased incentives for reciprocity. Hierarchical orders and centralized coordination also enforced uniformity and solidarity in Korean firms. Consequently, ILM-based employment practices have provided Korean firms with the advantages of speed for quickly imitating the competitors' behaviors. On the other hand, performance-oriented reward and evaluation practices have pushed Korean employees to work hard toward maximizing cost-efficiency. Employee flexibility practices such as outsourcing and the use of temporary workers have also contributed to improving cost-efficiency of Korean firms.

The competitive advantages Korean firms gained from this hybrid system are rapidly dissipating in a new competitive environment that requires innovation, change, and flexibility. Organizational innovation tends to progress by creating new knowledge, disseminating and sharing that knowledge throughout the firm, and integrating the knowledge embodied in individuals or groups into new products and services (Nonaka 1994). In rapidly changing dynamic environments, knowledge flow from external sources is critical for facilitating organizational innovation, enabling a firm to expand, refine, and modify its knowledge stock. By shortening the circulation period of current knowledge, dynamic environments push the organization not only to pursue experimentation for variation but also to challenge existing knowledge in relatively short product life cycles. In such environments, a nexus of HRM and organizational culture that emphasizes hierarchy and a short-term performance orientation may inhibit individual creativity and discourage employees to share and integrate their knowledge, negatively influencing organizational innovation for several reasons. First, a stock of firm-specific knowledge that is established through the operation of ILMs over a long horizon may easily become obsolete. Thus, dynamic environments are likely to limit the effectiveness of ILMs as external knowledge flow becomes a more important source of innovation. Second, a competitive compensation scheme draws the attention of managers away from long-term projects whose outcomes they may not be rewarded for. This shifts the attention of the firm towards a plethora of short-term R&D projects that deplete the long-term growth potential of these firms while keeping them in head-to-head competition within well-defined markets. A representative case is found in the initial failure of LG Electronics to respond to the iPhone in 2007 (Bae 2012). LG had achieved remarkable success in the feature phone segment, and instituted incentives for managers based on the number of feature phones they sold. Thus, managers had little incentive to deploy R&D towards smartphones. LG's firm-specific knowledge ended up working against it in a rapidly changing market.

Furthermore, the historical advantages posed by the hybrid system have been eroding. While performance-enhancing practices (relative performance evaluation and pay-for-performance) are effective for responding to immediate competitive pressures to improve performance, they may lead to a short-term performance orientation, intensive internal competition, and higher job-related stress. Employment flexibility practices also reduce the employee-employer interdependence and employees' trust toward each other and the organization. These effects have eroded the traditional advantages of the ILM-based model, so that the overall system is now saddled with the negative legacies of the ILM but also has lost the intra-company trust that it provided. The loss of trust has had a negative effect on organizational innovation by repressing employees' creative ideas, innovative behaviors, and knowledge exchange and integration.

A closely related problem is that the *chaebol* remain less capable of recruiting and motivating external hires. Such individuals are reluctant to adapt to the closed, male-dominant organizational cultures that continue to dominate the *chaebol*, and often fail to comprehend the structure of informal ties in which they are embedded. This failure gains importance when firms compete globally, and need to strike a balance between top-down global coordination and bottom-up responsiveness to local conditions. Continuing to exclude foreigners to some extent, along with women and other outsiders, the *chaebol* have had difficulty recruiting foreigners who are knowledgeable about their home markets. For example, a burgeoning interest in global talent management in the late 1990s drove a "global war for talent" (see Chapter 1 for details) among many firms across the world. In contrast, the *chaebol* employed local experts as the exception to a rule that favors Korean employees back at headquarters.

In summary, Korean firms have been using a unique HRM system that mixed a traditional ILM and a performance-oriented market system. This system supported the successful implementation of the fast-follower strategy by improving efficiency and speed. This same HRM system, however, is now an obstacle to Korean firms' pursuit of innovation by reducing creative ideas and cooperative behaviors. Furthermore, the HRM system and the associated organizational culture have played an important role in hindering the *chaebol* from recruiting skilled outsiders, especially those from other countries. Therefore, the challenge facing Korean firms is how to transform its HRM and organizational culture toward innovation, change, and flexibility.

Concluding remarks

Harnessing the fast-follower strategy through tight and comprehensive vertical integration and internal labor market based on loyalty and commitment, the *chaebol* have achieved speed and efficiency that has significantly contributed to their success in executing a fast-follower competitive strategy. While *chaebol* sticking to this traditional approach faced formidable challenges during the 1997 Asian Financial Crisis, many later transform themselves by introducing elements of the Anglo American capitalist system that emphasized flexibility and performance. Recently, Korean firms have been facing more serious structural challenges coming from new competitors from developing countries, armed with cost competitiveness (see Chapters 1 and 2). Simultaneously, these firms have been facing an uncertain, and turbulent business environment shaped by advances in information technology, digitalization, and open source innovation. These challenges strongly suggest that the fast-follower strategy will not be effective for the *chaebol* going forwards, and mandate them to put more emphasis on innovation, change, and flexibility. Our core contention is that the organizational structures, operational processes, and HRM strategies that the *chaebol* have adopted to support the fast-follower strategy have held them back in the new competitive environment, and that they will need to make their organizations more open, and learn how to partner and collaborate with other firms to successfully respond to fast-changing business environment and enhance their innovation capabilities. Only by doing so can Korea maintain its hard-won economic prosperity.

Notes

1 Fine, C.H., 1998. *Clockspeed: Winning industry control in the age of temporary advantage.* Perseus Books Readings, MA.
2 Lakhani, K., Hutter, K., Pokrywa, S.H., Füller, J., 2013. Open innovation at Siemens. Harvard Business School 9-613-100, June 17.
3 Handfield, R.B., Monczka, R.M., Giunipero, L.C., Patterson, J.L., 2009. *Sourcing and supply chain management.* 4th ed. (International ed.), South-Western.

References

Alakent, E., Lee, S., 2010. "Do institutionalized traditions matter during crisis? Employee downsizing in Korean manufacturing organizations." Journal of Management Studies 47 (3), 509–532.
Bae, J., 1997. "Beyond seniority-based systems: a paradigm shift in Korean HRM?" Asia Pacific Business Review 3 (4), 82–110.
Bae, J. 2012. "Smart phone as disruptive technologies: the case of LG electronics." SNU Business Case (the Institute of Management Research at Seoul National University).
Bae, J., Lawler, J.J., 2000. "Organizational and HRM strategies in Korea: impact on firm performance in an emerging economy." Academy of Management Journal 43 (3), 502–517.
Blasi, A., Puig, F., 2002. "Conditions for successful automation in industrial applications. A point of view." IFAC 15th Triennial World Congress, Barcelona, Spain.
Chang, S.J., 2008. Sony vs Samsung: The inside story of the electronics' giants battle for global supremacy. Singapore: John Wiley & Sons.
Chang, S.J., Hong, J. 2000. Economic performance of group-affiliated companies in Korea: Intragroup resource sharing and internal business transactions." Academy of Management Journal, 43: 429–448.
Fine, C.H., 1998. Clockspeed: Winning industry control in the age of temporary advantage. Perseus Books Readings, MA.
Handfield, R.B., Monczka, R.M., Giunipero, L.C., Patterson, J.L., 2009. Sourcing and supply chain management. 4th ed. (International ed.), South-Western.

Holstein, W.J., Nakarmi, L., 1995. "Korea". Business Week, July 31, Cover Story (online version).

Kang, S.-C., Yanadori, Y., 2011. "Adoption and coverage of performance-related pay during institutional change: An integration of institutional and agency theories." Journal of Management Studies, 48, 1837–1865.

Kim, W.C. 1986. "Global diffusion of the general trading company concept." Sloan Management Review (Summer): 35–43.

Kim, Dong-one and Seongsu Kim. 2003. "Globalization, Financial Crisis, and Industrial Relations: The Case of South Korea." Industrial Relations 42 (3), 341–367.

Kirk, D., 2001. "Technology; in Korea, broadband is part of the culture." New York Times, October 29 (online version).

Lakhani, K., Hutter, K., Pokrywa, S.H., Füller, J., 2013. "Open innovation at Siemens." Harvard Business School 9-613-100, June 17.

Lau, T.Y., Kim, S.W., Atkin, D., 2005. "An examination of factors contributing to South Korea's global leadership in broadband adoption." Telematics and Informatics 22 (4), 349–359.

Lee, K. 2013. Schumpeterian analysis of economic catch-up. Cambridge, UK: Cambridge University Press.

Lee, K., Bae, J., 2011. "SK Telecom and SK Networks: Designing corporate growth." SNU Business Case (the Institute of Management Research at Seoul National University).

Moon, H., 2016. The Strategy for Korea's Success. Oxford University Press.

Nonaka I., 1994. "A dynamic theory of organizational knowledge creation." Organization Science 5: 14–37.

Sarathy, R., 1985. "Japanese trading companies: Can they be copied?" Journal of International Business Studies (Summer): 101–119.

Shin, H., Lee, J., Kim, D., Rhim, H., 2015. "Strategic agility of Korean small and medium enterprises and its influence on operational and firm performance." International Journal of Production Economics 168, 181–196.

Song, J., Lee, K., 2014. The Samsung Way: Transformational management strategies from the world leader in innovation and design. McGraw-Hill.

Whitley, R., 1999. Divergent Capitalism: The Social Structuring and Change of Business System. New York: Oxford University Press.

4 SME productivity and export promotion policies in Korea[1]

Inchul Kim and Youngmin Kim

Globalization has had a significant bearing on the Korean economy, which achieved fast growth and development through outward-oriented strategies (see Chapter 1 of this volume). Exports as a proportion of GDP grew from 2.6 percent in 1960 to 53.9 percent in 2013. As economic growth has slowed in recent decades, exports have become ever more important to growth; while exports were responsible for 34.7 percent of GDP growth from 1981 to 1990, they were responsible for 98.1 percent from 2011 to 2015.[2] The *chaebol* have had substantial success riding globalization to penetrate international markets—a story told in Chapter 2 of this volume.

Yet, globalization has yet to benefit most small and medium-sized enterprises (SMEs). In 2013, SMEs constituted 99.9 percent of the number of firms and 87.5 percent of employment in Korea. The SME employment figure in Korea is remarkably high relative to the USA (43.6 percent), the UK (53.0 percent), Germany (62.5 percent), France (63.5 percent), Japan (76.1 percent), and the OECD average (67.0 percent). Indeed, this figure has steadily increased over time.[3] For this reason, the deterioration of SMEs' economic performance since the 1997 Asian Crisis has been a reason for concern. Despite their dominant share of the number of firms and employment, SMEs account only for 47.6 percent of total production and 49.5 percent of total value added. The output-per-worker productivity of SMEs fell from 35.4 percent of large enterprises LEs in 2000 to 29.6 percent by 2013.

Korean SMEs have performed particularly poorly in export markets, accounting for only 18.7 percent of total exports. Only 2.6 percent of 3.4 million SMEs were involved in exports in 2012, while 29.2 percent of 2,916 LEs engaged in exports.[4] In contrast, much larger proportions of SMEs exported in other OECD economies like Germany (11.3 percent), the Netherlands (10.1 percent), Italy (5.3 percent), and even the USA (4.0 percent). The dearth of exporting SMEs in Korea and their small export share are surprising as Korea is a highly export-oriented country. Even the SMEs that exported recorded low volume. As Figure 4.1 shows, 83.1 percent of exporting SMEs exported less than one million dollars a year and only 16.9 percent exported more than one million dollars per year.

As for firm dynamics, SMEs account for 31 percent and 26 percent of entries and exits from the export market, respectively, reflecting a high level of

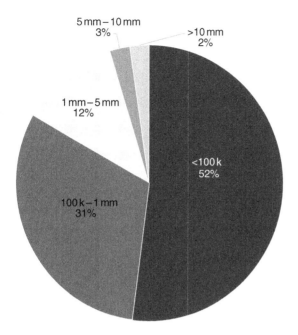

Figure 4.1 The structure of exporting SMEs by export value (US$).

volatility. The first-year survival rate for new SME exporters stood at 51 percent, while the three-year survival rate declined to 35 percent. That is, about half of new SME exporters are forced out of the export market within a year, and about two-thirds face the same fate within three years. However, once a firm survives over a three-year period, it enjoys a high probability of becoming a successfully globalized firm (Figure 4.2).

To investigate why SMEs have had such difficulty exporting, this chapter examines the relationship between SME exports and productivity. There is a virtuous cycle between exports and productivity. Firms that export can become more productive through learning in the export market, while more productive firms are more likely to have the competitiveness to export. Thus, understanding the relationship between exports and firm productivity becomes key to evaluating the efficacy of export promotion policies. In this chapter we provide some of the first empirical evidence on this virtuous cycle within the Korean context, finding that not only does SME productivity increase exports, but also that exports increase productivity. Together with analyses on SME exports and related policies, our findings identify ways to improve the export promotion support systems that the Korean government provides.

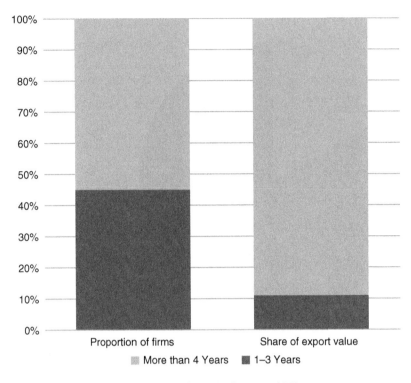

Figure 4.2 Share of exporting SMEs by operating year: 2012.

Globalization and productivity

Despite the importance of the relationship between globalization and productivity, there is insufficient understanding of two aspects of this relationship: (i) the productivity gap between globalized (exporting) and non-globalized (non-exporting) firms (the heterogeneity problem); and (ii) the potential bilateral causalities between globalization and productivity (the endogeneity problem). The existence of the productivity gap suggests that the marginal effect of globalization varies by productivity level, and policy-makers should adjust policy responses accordingly. The bilateral causalities require that we should verify and control endogeneity in the empirical analysis, and we should also be careful when interpreting the policy implications of the analysis. Although some studies have addressed one of the two issues, few have examined both simultaneously in the Korean context.[5]

The relationship between globalization and productivity can be characterized by the endogenous effect of productivity on globalization (the self-selection effect) and the effect of globalization on productivity (the learning effect). The former leads high productivity firms to pursue globalization, while the latter causes globalizing firms to achieve high productivity. Productivity leads to globalization as high-productivity firms are more likely to enter the international market than low-productivity firms because of their superior capabilities, and hence, lower costs of entering foreign markets.[6] It is widely accepted in most related studies using Korean data that the productivity-to-globalization causality exists. In contrast, there are relatively few analyses on the impact of globalization on productivity, and claims supporting the learning effects of globalization have received limited recognition. Hence, if we are to analyze causality between globalization and productivity, it is inevitably necessary to control the causality that runs the other way around.

Depending on the direction and magnitude of the endogenous causal relationships between globalization and productivity, industrial policies should either prioritize productivity over globalization or vice versa. If we can obtain policy implications from the empirical results, the implications could provide meaningful guidance for the Korean government in its comprehensive policy implementation of not only supporting globalization in general but also exports in particular. Before turning to our main empirical analysis on the relationship between export and productivity of SMEs, we first provide some background on Korea's export promotion policies targeted towards SMEs.

Export promotion policies for SMEs in Korea

Korea's economic development policies have long featured export promotion, designed to support firms when entering export markets and competing with foreign firms. From the early stages of its economic development, Korea has recognized the importance of international trade and achieved great success by pursuing an externally oriented development strategy. Given its past experiences, the Korean government has continued providing various forms of policy support to promote international trade. According to the WTO (2012, 20):

> Korea's general trade policy objective is to build a free and open economy based on market principles. [...] This has been to promote international competitiveness of its businesses and economic growth through openness and reforms.

Taking into account the high contribution of exports to growth and development, the government has strengthened export promotion policies for SMEs by reinforcing existing programs and introducing new ones.[7] The government's stance on SMEs has been quite generous in many aspects including finances, taxes, subsidies, employment, and of course, export promotion.[8] Overall government assistance for SMEs has remained strong.

As the structural gap between *chaebol*s and SMEs has increased since the 1997 Asian Crisis, the Korean government has shifted its policy focus from *chaebol*s to SMEs by increasing export support for SMEs at the expense of LEs. The government has kept promoting and supporting SME exports by implementing various policy measures designed solely for SMEs while letting large enterprises, including *chaebol*s, conduct their business in the overseas market with little official support.[9] As a result, both central and local governments and various government-backed trade-related organizations have expanded and diversified their export support systems for SMEs. Despite extensive governmental efforts, however, so far the overall evaluation of Korea's SME export promotion policies has turned out to be by no means as positive as the government expected.

Export promotion policies

The Korean government and related organizations have increased export promotion policies that are designed to adjust to development stages of SMEs and provided various forms of assistance to encourage as many non-exporting firms as possible to enter the export market. Well-known measures include tax incentives, duty drawbacks, favored policy loans, export finances, export insurance, free trade zones (FTZ), government-backed export support organizations,[10] business incubators, regional SME export marketing, FTA/export consulting support, and global business networks.[11] In 2013, the number of export promotion programs undertaken by the central and local governments and related organizations stood at 408, with a total budget of KRW 500 billion or more.[12] Compared with other major advanced economies, Korea provided more export support per US$1,000 GDP (Figure 4.3).[13]

This suggests that the role of SMEs in Korea, particularly in exports, is limited. The crucial questions that policy-makers need to ask are whether support

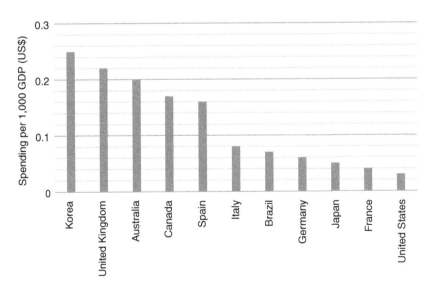

Figure 4.3 Estimated government export promotion spending of major trading countries: 2011.

systems have achieved their original policy goals, and if not, what kind of policy can respond efficiently to rapid changes in domestic and foreign economic and trade environments. A report published by the Ministry of Strategy and Finance (2014) suggests that Korean SME exporters have low levels of global capacity and competitiveness even with the assistance of policy support. The empirical analysis of the impact of financial assistance under current export promotion policies shows that government efforts contributed marginally to expanding the scale of SME exports over the short term, and have had little or no impact on export growth and financial performance. Also, business surveys by Lee et al. (2012) and Jang and Kim (2013) reported that SMEs' global capability and competitiveness remained unsatisfactory even after government support.

There are several problems with current export promotion policies. Financial support is centered exclusively on short-term performance, and the support system is loosely organized in a redundant and overlapping way without any comprehensive, systematic strategies (see Chapter 5 for details). Moreover, the system does not assess the capabilities of potential exporters, conduct ex post evaluations of policy support, or provide feedback afterward. The current export promotion policy system also faces criticism for inefficiency and lack of improvement. In contrast to such a trade policy that supposedly leans strongly towards market principles, the Korean government does not seem to hesitate to set policy goals and drive policy measures to achieve them (see Chapter 5). As a result, export promotion policies incur increasing social costs and fail to serve the purpose of realizing the globalization potential of SMEs. Furthermore, the government does not seem willing to reconsider quantity-based policies, at least for the time being. In 2013, the Ministry of Trade, Industry and Energy (MOTIE), which oversees export promotion policies, set goals to increase the trade volume from US$1 trillion in 2011 to US$2 trillion by 2020 and the number of exporting SMEs from 90,000 to 100,000 by 2017—and seems serious about achieving them.[14]

Noting these patterns, the OECD assessed government policies in Korea as "considerable policy activism" and suggested the "consolidation of policies and programmes" (OECD 2014b, 29):

> Korea is characterised by considerable policy activism. The number of policies and programmes is extremely large and their redesign and sometimes dissolution are frequent. Policies and programmes implemented abroad and considered benchmarks are regularly adopted in Korea. Indeed, few other countries create so many programmes and policies at such a pace. [...] Korea requires a period of programme consolidation. Any new initiatives need to be subject to thorough consideration of need, along with careful assessment of how they can be adapted to (rather than adopted in) Korea's specific circumstances.

Korea's export promotion policies ultimately aim to increase the number of exporting SMEs (and henceforth export volumes and benefits). This can be achieved only if the policies help firms enhance their productivity enough to enter and compete in overseas markets for higher profits that would be foregone otherwise.

Empirical analysis

The primary questions we ask are, "What is the marginal effect of exports on firm productivity distributed across productivity quantiles, controlling for endogeneity between the two factors?" and "What are the policy implications?" If the consequences of globalization differ by the distribution of productivity, then we can propose relevant policy solutions. Here, we present our empirical analysis and results.

This study used the *Survey of Business Activities* published annually by Statistics Korea (KOSTAT). It encompasses all Korean firms in every industry with 50 or more employees and gross capital of KRW 300 million (equivalent approximately to US$30,000) or more during 2006–2013. Given that the scope of the data includes business operations, finance, globalization, diversification, and systematization, the *Survey* provides sufficient information about the firms and their performances explored by our study on productivity and exports.

As highlighted earlier, we focused on productivity variations resulting from firm heterogeneity and endogeneity between productivity and exports. Variation in productivity across firms shows that there are many lower-productivity firms and fewer higher-productivity firms (in other words, a concentration of firms on the left side of the mean, with a right-skewed distribution and a long tail). This asymmetric distribution is observed for both exporting and non-exporting firms (Figure 4.4).

Although the distribution curves for the two groups of firms look similar at first glance, they significantly differ in one respect, with exporting firms tending to be more productive on average. Accordingly, we infer that globalization and related policies have different effects at different levels of productivity.

As the distribution of productivity is skewed to the right, a linear regression estimation based on mean values may risk distorting the effect of globalization on productivity, as such estimates cannot represent the distributional effects of globalization on productivity. Moreover, the effectiveness of policy support for globalization is likely to differ according to individual firms' productivity levels. Thus, it is necessary to consider the total productivity distribution and not confine the scope of analysis around the mean. Given this, we used the quantile regression model to estimate the effect of exports on productivity on productivity. This method divides firms into deciles of productivity distribution (labeled q10 to q90 in Table 4.1) and estimates the impact of globalization on productivity within each productivity quantile.[15] We also estimate the effects across separate years to account for year-specific variation.

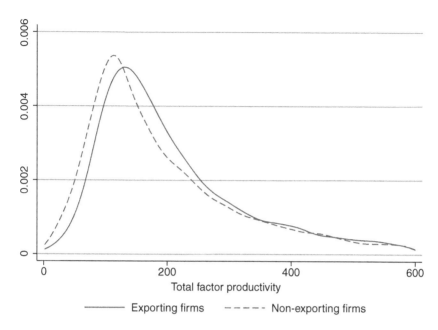

Figure 4.4 Productivity distributions of exporting and non-exporting firms: 2013.

Results and interpretations

The estimation found that exports enhance firm productivity for each and every year; the higher the productivity quantile, the smaller the export effect. Table 4.1 shows these results.

The gap in total factor productivity between exporting and non-exporting firms for 2006–2013 is widest at 52 percent in the 20th quantile, followed by 47 percent in the 50th quantile, and 39 percent in the 80th quantile. The result means that, controlling for endogeneity, exporting firms yield higher productivity than non-exporting firms in all productivity distribution, with the gap narrowing in higher quantiles. That is, the positive effect of globalization on productivity is prevalent but not identical for all firms that seek to transition themselves from non-exporting to exporting firms, as the gap is greater for firms with a lower level of productivity.

Note that this result only applies to firms that have survived long enough to achieve globalization successfully, and thus should not be used as a basis for prompting public policies to prioritize firms with low productivity (mostly SMEs). The self-selection process mentioned earlier implies that the chances of firms with low productivity achieving successful globalization on entering the export market are slim. As a result, export promotion policies are faced with a trade-off situation between the two conflicting options: a fair probability of success and low productivity growth by supporting high-productivity firms

Table 4.1 Quantile regression estimates of the effect of exports on firm productivity

Year	Quantiles								
	q10	*q20*	*q30*	*q40*	*q50*	*q60*	*q70*	*q80*	*q90*
2006	0.85**	0.86**	0.89**	0.79**	0.78**	0.71**	0.64**	0.58**	0.56**
	(0.07)	(0.07)	(0.05)	(0.04)	(0.04)	(0.04)	(0.05)	(0.06)	(0.04)
2007	0.79**	0.80**	0.76**	0.78**	0.75**	0.67**	0.64**	0.55**	0.50**
	(0.08)	(0.06)	(0.04)	(0.04)	(0.04)	(0.04)	(0.04)	(0.05)	(0.05)
2008	0.60**	0.67**	0.62**	0.64**	0.60**	0.57**	0.56**	0.53**	0.46**
	(0.04)	(0.05)	(0.04)	(0.05)	(0.04)	(0.04)	(0.05)	(0.06)	(0.07)
2009	0.51**	0.54**	0.51**	0.53**	0.52**	0.50**	0.50**	0.47**	0.50**
	(0.06)	(0.04)	(0.04)	(0.04)	(0.04)	(0.03)	(0.04)	(0.04)	(0.05)
2010	0.65**	0.64**	0.60**	0.56**	0.54**	0.54**	0.52**	0.52**	0.49**
	(0.04)	(0.04)	(0.04)	(0.03)	(0.03)	(0.03)	(0.04)	(0.05)	(0.07)
2011	0.53**	0.54**	0.52**	0.48**	0.49**	0.49**	0.49**	0.50**	0.44**
	(0.08)	(0.06)	(0.05)	(0.05)	(0.05)	(0.04)	(0.04)	(0.05)	(0.06)
2012	0.52**	0.58**	0.55**	0.50**	0.50**	0.49**	0.45**	0.48**	0.42**
	(0.04)	(0.03)	(0.04)	(0.03)	(0.03)	(0.03)	(0.04)	(0.04)	(0.05)
2013	0.34**	0.35**	0.34**	0.34**	0.32**	0.32**	0.29**	0.32**	0.33**
	(0.06)	(0.06)	(0.03)	(0.04)	(0.03)	(0.03)	(0.03)	(0.04)	(0.05)
2006– 2013	0.49**	0.52**	0.50**	0.48**	0.47**	0.44**	0.41**	0.39**	0.37**
	(0.03)	(0.02)	(0.02)	(0.02)	(0.01)	(0.02)	(0.02)	(0.02)	(0.02)

Source: Authors.

Notes
Standard errors are in parentheses.
** Significant at the 1 percent level.

versus a low probability of success and fair productivity growth by supporting low-productivity firms.

It is also important to note that this effect has become less important over time. As Figure 4.5 shows, this effect was prominent in 2006 but decreased in salience over time. Whether this decrease could be attributed towards short-term trends or a long-term change among Korean firms or global markets represents an important topic requiring additional study.

Discussion

According to the analysis, the success rate is low for non-exporting firms in the low productivity quantile seeking globalization. Nevertheless, once these firms have made a successful transition to globalization, they are likely to achieve relatively higher productivity gains. When new entrants to the export market overcome the low survival rate and operate over a long term, they can earn high export values, making significant contributions to the export market and

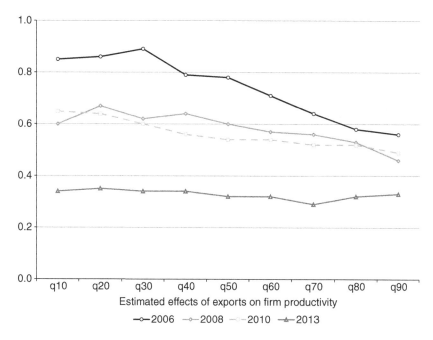

Figure 4.5 Effects of globalization on productivity by productivity quantile.

delivering increases in productivity. This indicates the need to tighten the policy process through which firms are evaluated and selected for their chance of survival in the export market based on growth potential, capability, and productivity. Also, once export support is granted through the assessment and selection process, it is desirable to provide support not for a short term but for a term long enough to ensure the survival of exporters over an extended period.

Policy implications

The findings of the analysis have several policy implications. First, policy support for the globalization of domestic businesses is essential to overcome economic restrictions inherent in the Korean local market as discussed in Chapter 1 and discover new growth drivers. Therefore, continuous policy efforts need be made to enhance the globalization of firms and henceforth productivity. The fact that only 2.6 percent of SMEs are exporters suggests that we can take advantage of a considerable opportunity. Policy changes, if properly designed and implemented, could result in realization of globalization's potential and social benefits. What is needed is to focus on improving and complementing export-oriented policies. In particular, identifying SMEs with strong potential and encouraging them to join the export market would pave the way for successful globalization. Given this, it is necessary to enhance the capability assessment of exporting firms eligible for policy support. This applies to both new entrants and incumbents in the export market. SMEs displaying high productivity and strong capability before and after their entry into the export market are likely to survive and make fundamental contributions to boosting overall productivity at both the industrial and national level by way of exports.

Second, it is necessary to adjust the support period for exporting firms based on their stages and enhance ex post management of follow-up support. The transition into the export market is not easy for firms specializing in the domestic market. It is even more challenging for new entrants to survive successfully beyond an extended period, as it takes time for new entrants to take root in the export market, survive as an exporter, and show reliable results. Policy support over a fixed period should help new entrants in the export market overcome uncertainties in their transition to becoming globalized firms. Accordingly, it is necessary to consider extending policy support beyond the entry stage to include the post-entry period. However, it is desirable to set a sunset clause or a cap on policy support. This way, time-bound policy commitments clearly indicate a specific policy direction and time horizon, and thus reduce the risk of unnecessary waste of socially valuable resources such as time, money, policy efforts, and so on.

Third, the export support system should be simplified, streamlined, and made more flexible to increase efficiency. It is vital to formulate a diverse range of policy support as rapid changes in the forms and methods of globalization often create insurmountable hurdles for many firms, especially SMEs. However, the current export support system is likely to be redundant and wasteful because of duplicated efforts by several policy bodies working in similar ways (see Chapter 5 in this volume for details). They should be consolidated to streamline and operate the export support system flexibly. Moreover, it may be a good idea to designate an oversight organization to manage and evaluate the overall implementation process. It is still necessary to pursue the economies of scope by ensuring diversity in the objects (SMEs) of export support.

This study found that the industrial policy for globalization is set to mitigate information asymmetry and entry costs—key factors considered by firms in their decision to enter the export market. The likelihood of achieving industrial policy objectives increases only when potential participants in the economy can make decisions in a socially desirable manner. Assuming the same goes for globalization, we can define socially desirable economic globalization as a process that encourages the self-selection of firms with high potential to enter the export market while discouraging firms with limited potential from going global. That is, it is important to design export promotion policies in a way that reduces information asymmetry and entry costs by providing information on the export market, competition, and globalization while enabling businesses to decide on globalization based on their own potential, which benefits not only the firms to avoid making wrong decisions but also the society from wasting resources.

Global value chains as an alternative approach

Meanwhile, aside from providing direct support for SMEs to become exporters, it is necessary to apply the export support system to indirect exports, which takes place through the supply of intermediary goods to other exporters. Given that SMEs face relatively high uncertainties and substantial fixed costs in their entrance to the export market, they can contribute to exports by aligning their value chain with those of existing exporters (LEs, other SMEs, and foreign direct investment companies) or taking part in the global value chain, rather than by pursuing direct globalization or participating in the export market directly. Accordingly, it is necessary to consider ways to increase the benefits of exportation by expanding the scope of export support systems to include indirect exports.[16]

There is an imperative need to reinterpret the global value chain (GVC) from the perspective of globalization, productivity, and industrial policy, as the global value chain is becoming critical to redefining the methods and benefits of globalization.[17] Under the global value chain, a firm's productivity is affected not by individual performance but also the collective performance of all participants in the value chain. In other words, the productivity of a firm depends on which partners it works with as well as the firm's value chain (see Chapter 3 for more details). Apart from a firm's direct participation in the export market, the contribution of its value added to exports throughout the global value chain is increasingly important. Even if the export value is the same, the value added by exports significantly varies, creating a different impact on the productivity of firms. Accordingly, it is necessary to consider industry policies that induce participation in the value chain in Korea and abroad.

Notes

1 This chapter is an abridged version of "Changes in Globalization and Productivity in the Korean Industry and Industrial Policy Implications", published in 2015 by the Korean Institute for Industrial Economics and Trade, in which more extensive arguments can be found.
2 Bank of Korea, ECOS database.
3 See OECD (2015), Figure 2.5 and Table 1.2, 29.
4 Kim et al. (2014), 56.
5 See discussions in Aw et al. (2000), Hahn (2005), Kim et al. (2014), and Kim and Kim (2015), for example.
6 See Melitz's (2003) seminal paper on this line of argument.
7 See The Committee for the Sixty-Year History of the Korean Economy (2010), for example.
8 OECD (2014a), 15.
9 After the Asian Crisis, the Korean government started to restructure and regulate LEs harshly instead of supporting them.
10 The organizations include the Korea Trade Promotion Corporation, Korea International Trade Association, Small & Medium Business Corporation, etc., for instance.
11 See Mah (2010) and Sakong and Koh (2010) for an extensive explanation for various forms of export promotion policies in Korea.

12 The central government supported only 60 of the 408 total export promotion policies in 2013, compared against 301 supported by local governments and an additional 47 supported by government-backed organizations. Policies supported by the central government, however, tended to be substantially larger, accounting for 302 billion KRW in support of the 513.5 billion KRW total (Cho et al. 2014: 60). These figures exclude export finance support (export credit loans), for which data are not available.

13 As Figure 4.3 suggests, Korea is hardly alone in supporting SME exports. See Kim et al. (2014) for more details on the SME export promotion by the USA, Japan, Germany, and Finland.

14 See Ministry of Trade, Industry and Energy (2013, 2016).

15 This method can produce a more comprehensive picture of the export effects, because it needs not assume a constant marginal effect over the entire productivity distribution. Hence, it has an analytical advantage over the conventional mean regression models. Particularly, when the productivity distribution, an object of the analysis, is asymmetric, the quantile regression model is useful to estimate its marginal effect more accurately than mean regressions. Moreover, we controlled the potential endogeneity between productivity and exports by instrumental variables (IV) methods. See Kim and Kim (2015) and Koenker (2005) for more extensive arguments.

16 Oh (2013) estimated that the overall indirect exports by non-exporting manufacturing SMEs in Korea could reach 102 percent of direct exports in 2009.

17 We can see the GVC as another interpretation of indirect exports, but it has a much wider scope than indirect exports and involves far more players and complexity.

References

Aw, Bee Yan, Sukkyun Chung, and Mark J. Roberts. 2000. "Productivity and Turnover in the Export Market: Micro-Level Evidence from the Republic of Korea and Taiwan (China)." World Bank Economic Review 14(1): 65–90.

Cho, Youngsam, Youngjoo Lee, and Chang Yong Han. 2014. Policy Suggestions for Efficient Export Supporting System for SMEs. Seoul: Korea Institute for Industrial Economics and Trade [in Korean].

Committee for the Sixty-Year History of the Korean Economy. 2010. The Korean Economy: Six Decades of Growth and Development, Volume III. Foreign Trade. Seoul: The Committee for the Sixty-Year History of the Korean Economy [in Korean].

Hahn, Chin Hee. 2005. "Exporting and Performance of Plants: Evidence from Korean Manufacturing." In International Trade in East Asia, ed. Takatoshi Ito and Andrew K. Rose. Chicago: The University of Chicago Press, 53–80.

Jang, Sangsik, and Yemin Kim. 2013. "Recent SMEs Export Activities and Policy Suggestions to Expand Exports." Trade Focus, February 2013. Seoul: Institute for International Trade [in Korean].

Kim, Jeong Gon, Bo-Young Choi, Boram Lee, and Minyoung Lee. 2014. Major Countries' Policies for Supporting Internationalization of SMEs and Their Implications. Sejong: Korea Institute for International Economic Policy [in Korean].

Kim, Inchul, and Youngmin Kim. 2015. Changes in Globalization and Productivity in the Korean Industry and Industrial Policy Implications. Sejong: Korea Institute for Industrial Economics and Trade [in Korean].

Koenker, Roger. 2005. Quantile Regressions. New York: Cambridge University Press.

Lee, Youngjoo, Dongjin Yoon, Youngseop Shim, and Hyejin Jin. 2012. "An Empirical Study of the Success Factors of Korean Global Hidden Champion and Respective Policy Issues." Seoul: Korea Institute for Industrial Economics and Trade [in Korean].

Mah, Jai S. 2010. "Export Promotion Policies, Export Composition and Economic Development in Korea." Paper presented at Law and Development Institute Inaugural Conference, Sydney, Australia, October 16.

Melitz, Marc J. 2003. "The Impact of Trade on Intra-Industry Reallocations and Aggregate Industry Productivity." Econometrica 71(6): 1695–1725.

Ministry of Strategy and Finance. 2014. "An Evaluation of Export-Supporting Programs and Performance Enhancing Schemes." Sejong: Ministry of Strategy and Finance [in Korean].

Ministry of Trade, Industry and Energy. 2016. "Trade Volume Two Trillion Dollars by 2020" [in Korean]. Accessed March 7. http://motie.go.kr/motie/ne/presse/press2/bbs/bbsView.do?bbs_seq_n=72250&bbs_cd_n=81.

Ministry of Trade, Industry and Energy. 2013. "Export Promotion Policies for Small and Medium Enterprises and High Potential Enterprises." Sejong: Ministry of Trade, Industry and Energy [in Korean].

Ministry of Trade, Industry and Energy. 2014. "A Promotion Policy for Globalization of Domestic Firms." Sejong: Ministry of Trade, Industry and Energy [in Korean].

Ministry of Trade, Industry and Energy. 2015. 2015 Foreign Trade and International Commerce Policies. Sejong: Ministry of Trade, Industry and Energy [in Korean].

Oh, Dongyoon. 2013. A Study on Estimation of SMEs' Indirect Exports. Seoul: Korea Small Business Institute [in Korean].

Organisation for Economic Cooperation and Development. 2014a. OECD Economic Survey Korea – Overview. Paris: Organisation for Economic Cooperation and Development.

Organisation for Economic Cooperation and Development. 2014b. OECD Reviews on Innovation Policy: Industry and Technology Policies in Korea. Paris: Organisation for Economic Cooperation and Development.

Organisation for Economic Cooperation and Development. 2015. Entrepreneurship at a Glance 2015. Paris: Organisation for Economic Cooperation and Development.

Sakong, Il, and Youngsun Koh, eds. 2010. The Korean Economy: Six Decades of Growth and Development. Seoul: Korea Development Institute.

Small and Medium Business Administration. 2015. Statistics for SMEs. Daejeon: Small and Medium Business Administration [in Korean].

Small and Medium Business Administration. 2013. "A Policy for Strengthening SMEs Export Capabilities." Daejeon: Small and Medium Business Administration [in Korean].

U.S. Trade Promotion Coordinating Committee. 2012. 2012 National Export Strategy: Powering the National Export Initiative, Year 3. Washington, D.C.: U.S. Trade Promotion Coordinating Committee.

World Trade Organization. 2012. Trade Policy Review, Report by the Secretariat – Republic of Korea. Geneva: World Trade Organization.

5 South Korean SMEs and the quest for an innovation economy

Michelle F. Hsieh

The dominant account in understanding the successful catch-up of the East Asian tigers has focused on state capacities for nurturing new industries by inducing private firms into areas they would otherwise not enter, investing in managerial and technological capabilities and enlarging their scale and scope. This process created large firms with substantial organizational capabilities, with the Korean *chaebol* as the exemplar (Amsden 1989; Amsden and Chu 2003; Evans 1995). Yet, while the developmental state created large-scale firms, it simultaneously retarded the development and growth of small and medium-sized enterprises (SMEs) by systematically funneling capital and business opportunities towards national champions, as Chapter 1 described in more detail.

Yet, the SME sector has become increasingly important for a country's future prospects. For a country to stay ahead, the state needs to develop a concrete set of ties with the private sector to induce growth of new firms (the so-called embedded thesis) and develop new and innovative industries. The transformation often requires decentralized and flexible state policies and flexible firms to respond and adapt to the rapidly changing global environment and to develop cutting-edge technological capacities continuously to stay ahead. Essentially, the new developmental project is about exploring state-society linkages that are conducive to innovation, such as "embedded autonomy" (Evans 1995), "governed interdependence" (Weiss 1998), or the "developmental network state" (Ó Riain 2004; Block 2008; Block and Keller 2011; Negoita and Block 2012). As Chapter 4 described, such linkages are particularly salient with respect to SMEs, which can lack the independent resources commanded by larger firms.

Korea is a case in point. Korea's response to globalization and competition from other latecomers has been to keep pace with the technology race by developing various innovation-driven regional clusters in the 2000s and cultivating SME entrepreneurship, going beyond the existing emphasis and dependence on *chaebol*-led innovation. The policies may have changed slightly in the past three administrations but the central thrust remains what has been called "balanced national development" and cultivating SMEs and networks among them to enhance learning and innovation. Essentially, the various regional innovation programs aim to bring closer collaborations among SMEs, universities, and government-funded research institutes (GRI) by housing them in innovation complexes. A key question that motivates the research here is: Under what circumstances can a system of SMEs become competitive in exports, R&D, and investment in international rather than just domestic markets (see also Chapter 4)? Thus, in this chapter, I focus on the SME sectors that have potential both in innovation and in exports, given that export performance is vital to Korea's economic well-being. For these sectors, this chapter aims to provide an assessment of various regional innovation cluster and SME-based entrepreneurship initiatives.

This chapter is organized as follows: first, I will summarize the legacy of the Korean *chaebol*-dominant industrial system and contextualize Korea's current regional innovation clustering initiatives. Second, I will provide a preliminary assessment of the outcomes of these innovation clusters and the rationales behind them from my research. Third, a section will be devoted to discussing the transformation of the other well-known network-based economy, Taiwan, and its transformation in the SME-based machinery sectors to illustrate the alternative approach to the innovation quest. The comparison with the Taiwanese experience serves to illuminate the prospects and obstacles in moving from a *chaebol*-dominated economy to creating an innovation and network-based economy in Korea.

The Korean transition to an innovation economy: SME-based entrepreneurship and innovation clusters

Conventional wisdom attributes the underdevelopment of Korean SMEs to the government's overly strong support of the *chaebol* and pays only lip service to the SME constituents. However, there is ample evidence indicating that numerous programs to support SMEs were established in the 1980s and have accelerated since the 2000s, especially by the Ministry of Commerce, Industry, and Energy (MOCIE). Moreover, revitalizing SME-based entrepreneurship and SME innovation policies, as expressed in various regional innovation programs, occurred in the context of balanced national development and decentralization that aimed to delegate power to the regional government during the 2000s (Park and Koo 2013; Lee 2009; Hassink 2001). These initiatives, however, as I will demonstrate, have actually hindered the development of SME-based entrepreneurship. The following section will discuss the limitations of the state-led development legacy in which a similar pattern of state support has thrived in the quest for innovation economy in the past decade. I will first discuss the dynamics of these state initiatives and then use a detailed study of the Gyeonggi province's programs to illustrate the problems.

SME policy prior to the 1997 financial crisis

In the early 1980s, the government instituted a series of measures designed to curb the overdominance of the *chaebols* and the imbalanced development resulting from the heavy industrialization drive. Policies favoring the growth of SMEs can be summed up in two areas: preferential financing for SMEs and the promotion of technology-driven sectors through systemization of the subcontracting program between assemblers and suppliers (Lim 1998). These measures aimed at revitalizing and strengthening SMEs, especially the suppliers of components to larger firms, but had mixed results. One might expect that the state might rely on the same mechanisms that led to their earlier success supporting the rise of the *chaebol*. Indeed, preferential financing programs helped chosen SMEs grow into mini-*chaebols*, instead of developing a vibrant parts sector as a whole. Second, the systemization of the subcontracting program, instead of helping the parts makers to develop, further locked them into overdependence on a single assembler and created vulnerability (Hsieh 2011).

In essence, the Korean path to technology learning and industrial development prior to the 1997 financial crisis was associated with policies of picking national champions where firm-specific policies (in the context of the nexus of the Korean state and large *chaebols*) prevailed. The legacies of past development strategies led to the underdevelopment of entrepreneurship and technological capabilities of Korean SMEs in several ways. First, state intervention tended to further concentrate production. Second, it emphasized volume and the assembly of finished goods, which broadly advantaged the *chaebol* over SMEs. Third, the approach of picking winners and providing firm-specific support policies undermined potential inter-firm collaborations, making SMEs prioritize the development of a vertical relationship with the state or with *chaebol* over horizontal cooperation with other SMEs. These factors largely explain the ambivalent outcomes of 1980s-era policies in developing the parts sector and cultivating SME-based entrepreneurship.

Post-1998 cluster-based SME policy

Since the early 2000s, Korea has aimed to respond to rapid global changes and to move away from investment-driven industrial policies and to diffusion-oriented and capability-building innovation ones by tapping into the idea of regional innovation systems. In light of the successful transformation of regions such as Silicon Valley, Baden-Württemberg in Germany, and Emilia Romagna in Italy to withstand global competition since the 1980s, many regions in advanced countries have set up science parks and innovative supporting agencies (Saxenian 1994; Herrigel 1996; Powell 1990; Lazerson 1995; Piore and Sabel 1984), instituting a cluster-oriented development agenda that aims to build connections among firms in the same geographic location. Clusters and networks are important for innovation on the basis of the assumption that social networking helps to transmit knowledge and information and is thus conducive to generating new ideas. Therefore, networks of social relations embedded in a geographical region are believed to be conducive to innovation, as geographical proximity tends to encourage face-to-face interaction, which strengthens inter-firm relationships and favors information exchange, learning, and knowledge production, the key to sustaining future economic growth and development (Saxenian and

Hsu 2001; Powell, Koput, and Smith-Doerr 1996; Smith-Doerr and Powell 2005; Castilla et al. 2000). Based on this idea, Korea has pushed for networking and the diffusion of ideas, as manifested in regional innovation clustering initiatives. Moreover, the clustering initiatives also involve connecting the private firms with research intensive agencies such as government research institutes (GRIs) and universities to generate value added in a more decentralized setting in the quest to a knowledge economy.

To realize the goal of balanced national development, regional innovation initiatives such as clustering polices were the new direction for regional development in Korea under Roh's administration (2003–2008) that strove to move beyond the prior dirigiste development approach and devolve powers onto regions. Hence, building industrial innovation clusters has been a dominant narrative in Korea over the last decade. For instance, existing industrial complex programs[1] (which focused mainly on production functions) were transferred to regional innovation clusters that were intended to construct an ecosystem with linkages among firms, universities, and GRIs that would be conducive to innovation.[2] The number of nationally designated industrial clusters has moved from the initiative stage of seven designated pilot innovative clusters in 2005 to 12 national designated complexes in 2007 to subsequently over 193 regional industrial complexes since 2010, under the industrial innovation cluster programs (ICCP) (Lee 2009; MKE and KICOX 2011, 9). The programs were further expanded to various types of hub and spoke clusters (referring to the ways in which different clusters are connected) and mini-clusters within the industrial complex from 2010, during the Lee administration (2008–2013).[3] Over 36,000 companies were chosen in the cluster programs by 2011 (MKE and KICOX 2011). In addition to the nationally devised regional innovation clustering programs, the regional strategic industries program encouraged and supported all 13 provincial regions for each region to select and promote its own strategic industries by establishing techno parks and specialized R&D zones (Kim, Lee, and Hwang 2014; Lee 2012).

In addition to MOCIE's clustering polices, the Ministry of Science and Technology (MOST) promoted research activities and boosted innovation and technology learning by constructing numerous R&D clusters. For example, chosen firms were granted R&D subsidies (on average one billion won) to set up research labs to collaborate with local universities and another four billion won for research projects every year. Consequently, the R&D clusters flourished; the number of recipient institutions went from 41 institutions covering six technology areas in 2004 to 103 institutions in 13 technology areas in 2007 (Lee 2012, 161).

All in all, as one interviewee put it, "clusters are booming business in Korea" (interview Park2, GSBC 2012). So, is Korea becoming a networked/clustered nation? Despite efforts to build bottom-up innovation clusters that were needed for the rapid innovation quest, the Korean experience suggests mixed outcomes for the initiatives. The reality is that Korean clusters do not necessarily generate the positive outcomes envisioned by the agglomeration theorists, nor are they a panacea to boosting national competitiveness and innovation capacities.

The various innovation clustering initiatives by the Korean local and national governments ended up creating clusters that have no synergy effect. In the following, I will draw on existing research and my own research on the case study of Gyeonggi Province's regional innovation programs to illustrate the inherent problems.

Limits of state-led regional innovation initiatives: generating homogenous institutions across regions

To start with, these so-called regional initiatives actually consist of nationally devised and implemented policies. Despite emphasis on decentralization in the SME-oriented innovation policy, programs such as techno parks and research consortiums remained strongly national, as provinces had only the role of co-financing the initiatives created by the central government (Hassink 2004). Instead of empowering regions, these initiatives generated homogenous institutions that did not respond to local demands. For instance, the nationally designated techno parks were too homogenous in terms of their aims and targeted groups instead of linking well to the endogenous characteristics of the regions where they were situated (Hassink 2001, 1388). In other cases, over 20 regional bio-clusters were designated by MOCIE as a result of the bio-industry promotion policy, but most were for low-tech and low value-added regional agricultural and marine products (Lee 2009, 363). A researcher involved in evaluating clustering projects remarked, "I think that the regional clustering program was not so successful because I think we selected too many clusters. In order to succeed, you know the economies of scale are very critical" (Interview B Lee 2012). Another interviewee's remark also captures the problem: "The regional initiatives actually replicated mini national bureaucracies across all provinces but they lacked appropriate manpower to execute the programs. As a result, resources were dissipated" (Interview Jung 2015).

The immediate consequences of these nationally devised regional policies actually generated competition among these actors (i.e., regional governments) to seek more power and resources from the central government, which "resulted in a glut of institutions," as Lee describes it (2009, 362). The experience of Gyeonggi Province's regional innovation programs is a case in point. Gyeonggi Province is considered to have the densest innovation support infrastructure of all the provinces in Korea. It holds high R&D potential in various statistical measures, in terms of number of R&D workers, number of jobs in the high technology sector, and numerous independent, innovative SMEs in the electronics and machinery sectors (Hassink 2004, 163). As a strong manufacturing base, Gyeonggi Province has the largest Science and Technology (S&T) budget among all Korean provinces (Chung 1999). Yet, a lion's share of the budget was devoted to co-financing these nationally devised clustering initiatives (Hassink 2004) or generating policies that ran parallel to the national programs. For instance, the province set up its own intermediary agencies, such as the GSBC (Gyeonggi Small and Medium Business Center) and the Gyeonggi Institute of

Science and Technology Promotion (GSTEP) to work with SMEs in high-tech sectors. The services consisted of varieties of small business incubation, start-up programs, and R&D support to promote technology and innovation in Gyeonggi Province (Interview info).

When the programs are examined in detail, however, the regional initiatives of Gyeonggi Province share similarities to their equivalent national counterparts, such as SBC (Small and Medium Business Corporation), SMBA (Small and Medium Business Administration), and STEPI (Science and Technology Policy Institute), the national agencies that assist SMEs and promote science and technological development. For instance, as stated on the GSTEP website, one of its primary orientations is to support industrial cluster innovation programs in Gyeonggi Province.[4] It aims to strengthen cooperation among industries, academia, and research industries within strategically targeted industries, and it developed 14 IICC (Industry Innovation Cluster Committees) operating institutions within Gyeonggi Province (Interview W Lee 2012). In many ways, these programs were parallel to aspects of the national Industrial Complex Cluster Program (ICCP), such as the hub and spoke and mini-clusters.

The GSBC, established in 1996, promotes business start-ups, provides technology and marketing support to individual firms that connect SMEs with international buyers and organizes trade delegations and trade fairs. Interviews with the relevant personnel at GSBC and SBC and studying their official documents suggest that GSBC, SBC, and SMBA (the latter two have branches in Gyeonggi Province) provide similar support programs to SMEs in Gyeonggi Province.

In addition to generating an excessive number of institutions, there is a lack of inter-organizational coordination and exchange among these regional cluster initiatives, which contradicts the idea that regional clustering would encourage the kind of coordination and information exchange seen in the European experience (Hassink 2004). On a visit I made to SBC Gyeonggi Branch, which is located in the same complex as GSBC, when I asked the interviewees at SBC Gyeonggi Branch about their relationship with GSBC and the services they provided, an interviewee replied, "Actually we do not have much relationship with GSBC. Because it's a regional government performance organization, and we are the national government performance organization, ..." The interviewee further acknowledged that GSBC and SBC are competing organizations (Interviewee SBC 2012). Another interviewee at GSBC (a policy analyst) raised the question of an ongoing debate about whether SBC or GSBC should be the medium for the clustering programs (Interview GSBC 2012c).

Not only did supporting institutions not interact with each other, my interviews with and visits to various Gyeonggi Province clustering support agencies, such as GSBC and the well-regarded Pangyo Techno Valley initiative,[5] revealed that many synergies have been realized despite the amount of resources that have been invested. Pangyo Techno Valley is considered one of the most successful cluster initiatives among them all, for the revenue the firms located inside the techno park generated exceeds 70 trillion won (about $60 billion US) annually. This amount accounts for over 20 percent of the annual gross domestic product

(GDP) of the Gyeonggi Province, the largest Korean province, and is equivalent to the GDP of Busan Region (interview Pangyo 2015; *Korean Herald*, 2016/04/07).[6] Even with such a stellar performance, policy-makers acknowledged that there seemed to be little networking among firms (Interviews GSBC 2012c; W Lee 2012; Pangyo Valley 2012; 2015; GSTEP 2015). There are factors independent of clustering initiatives that may have resulted in the rapid growth of Pangyo Techno Valley; they include its close geographical proximity to Metropolitan Seoul, which attracts Korean conglomerates and multinationals (MNCs) (Interview Jung 2015).

Most interviewees acknowledged that varieties of clustering programs did not generate the kind of networking and synergies that policy-makers had envisioned. Firms located inside these innovation clusters and in GSBC incubation programs did not interact very much, contrary to what the initiatives and theories had predicted. The remark from a GSBC interviewee illustrates the reasons behind the lack of interaction in the clustering initiatives and the dilemma they faced:

> Firms come to the industrial cluster to take advantage of government incentives as opposed to working with each other. The government induces companies to form clusters with supporting money and research funds.... The real question here is whether the government should be the one constructing clusters.
>
> (Interview GSBC 2012c)

In short, despite the attempts to develop bottom-up innovation initiatives, the Korean innovation system remains national in its characteristics. For one, the top-down approach has generated homogenous and excessive innovation support agencies that provide services that do not respond to regional demands. At the same time, most provinces remain dependent on the financial support of the national government to manage these programs, and lack the capacity to coordinate either these national initiatives or the local and regional initiatives. Second, the top-down regional innovation initiatives create horizontal coordination problems. For the provinces that have more manpower and resources, such as Gyeonggi province, the regional support agencies actually overlap with the support infrastructure of the national agencies, such as SMBA and SBC. Thus, support programs are fragmented and often redundant as opposed to being complementary. The case study of Gyeonggi province's SME supporting programs illustrates inter-agency and inter-firm competition instead of cooperation. Third, the specific scheme of R&D subsidies and incentives created by the government induces firms to come to the clusters to take advantage of government perks but not to do networking. Horizontal coordination and collaboration among firms remain far from being realized. Consequently, the state-led regional innovation policies have led to rent-seeking instead of innovation-seeking behavior on the part of agencies and firms and to competition among regions and firms to receive endorsement and support.

Constructing ties with university, industry, and public research institutes

The varieties of regional innovation cluster programs connect the private sector, especially the SMEs, with research-oriented actors, such as universities and GRIs, for R&D. The emphasis on regional universities and GRIs for local R&D can be distinguished from the past industrial complex program that mainly served to house manufacturers and suppliers in a geographical compound. Most interviewees involved in clustering evaluation and planning concurred that Korean cluster programs are about connecting universities with *individual firms* (emphasis added, Interview KOSBI 2012): "The main mission of techno parks is to provide some kind of linkages between R&D experts and SMEs" (Interview B Lee 2012) and "They have universities focusing on technology development in the clusters" (Interview GSBC2 2012).

The Korean vision of connecting different actors is about developing customized support by bridging individual SMEs with different resources they can tap into to succeed in the global market. Various supporting programs under the Creative Economies Project of the current Park administration illustrate this kind of customized winner takes all support.[7] For example, *Business Korea* reports the extensive supports received by a marine bio company that succeeded in breaking into the US market:

> This company built a factory with a cloud fund of 80 million won from 43 investors after it developed cosmetic products using fishery byproducts with support from the Jeonnam Creative Economy Center. Marine Techno Co. is now receiving various support including small and medium innovation, laws, financial consulting and other professional areas beyond simple funding from the Creative Economy Center.
>
> (*Business Korea*, May 3, 2016)[8]

In a site visit to Pangyo Creative Economy Center, similar kinds of support were mentioned as being offered to chosen start-ups (interview Pangyo 2015).[9]

In addition to the integrated and comprehensive one-stop support programs by Creative Economy Innovation Centers, different government agencies, at both the national and regional levels, offer similar most-promising innovative SME program awards to individual SMEs, such as SMBA's global hidden champion programs, KICOX's global leading companies program, and regional programs such as GSBC's entrepreneurial incubation programs (Interview GSBC Park 2012). To give a few examples: The global leading companies program by the Korean Industrial Complex Corporation (KICOX), the national agency in overseeing innovation cluster programs, aspires to take all measures to help the selected promising firms (as poster children of KICOX) to become global leading firms.[10] According to the news release by KICOX, the winners will receive customized growth support in overall business activities from building factories to overseas expansion, including industrial complex location support and personal company doctor consulting, to a collective company growth support platform project operated by KICOX with an exclusive platform manager and any other support and services the companies might need that were not included in the program. Catering to the program will be as exhaustive as possible with the help of networks of related organizations. Moreover, the selected companies will receive All-In-One financial support services from financial institutions (i.e., Shin-A Bank), including prime interest loans and support for technological evaluation fees, direct investment, and overseas expansion.[11]

At the regional level, close scrutiny of the aforementioned mini-cluster programs, in which innovation clusters are organized through the alliances of industry (consisting of large firms and SMEs), universities, and research institutions according to the specific industry or technology field, also reveals limited impacts of constructing cross-cutting ties, despite their acclaimed success compared with all other clustering initiatives. For instance, the GSTEP interviewee pointed out that the mini-cluster for an intelligent electronics device (a robotic cleaning machine) seemed to work well compared with other mini-clusters, but he also acknowledged that it was a privately initiated cluster (Interview W Lee 2012). Another success story of a mini-cluster is an electronic/intelligent rice cooker that has already gained a foothold in the international market (Interview W Lee 2012). But the growth of these two cases was merely captured by an individual firm in the industry and did not cascade to other firms.

Other government R&D clustering and support programs show similar findings regarding the building capability of individual firms rather than any development of collaboration and diffusion. The current progress concurs with a previous study that revealed a fragmented consortium structure as Korean firms hesitated to cooperate with one another (Sakakibara and Cho 2002, 656) despite continued efforts from the government to foster innovation programs by connecting the private sector with GRIs and universities. The earlier research findings suggest that 78 out of 190 consortiums had two participants; also, many companies were included, as universities and national research institutes count as consortium participants (ibid., 685). Evaluating the programs after a decade-long effort of decentralization and constructing cross-cutting ties among different actors, my research findings suggest that these clusters and R&D cluster programs have continued to generate "infrastructure" support for individual firms as opposed to creating a "system" that supports a network of firms. For instance, in evaluating the R&D clustering programs, most interviewees acknowledged not having witnessed a substantial synergy effect as of 2015. They noted difficulties in getting people together to form a research consortium (Interview W Lee 2012). In particular, consortiums led by universities were not successful, in spite of what the plan had predicted.

As comprehensive and ambitious as these support programs are for nurturing world-class Korean SMEs, these measures are most likely to be successful in growing individual firms, without any spillover effects. An interviewee who was involved in evaluating innovative SME applications pointed to the inherent problems of the initiatives:

Firms are more interested in getting the government resources to solve their own problems as opposed to working with each other in an R&D consortium. Collaboration is that not good; they compete to work with public research institutes in order to get R&D subsidies and solve their own problems.

(Interview Song 2012)

In fact, of all the regional innovation initiatives, most interviewees thought that the program that worked best was the techno doctor program for solving the specific problems of individual firms (Interviews, B Lee 2012; GSBC Park 2012; Oh 2012). For instance, the GSBC connected individual experts, either retired engineers or researchers with individual firms, to help solve problems (Interview GSBC Park 2012).

To sum up: to date, research suggests that the Korean regional innovation initiatives generate customized capability building programs for individual chosen firms. They do not, however, generate the kind of institutional embeddedness and thickness that the network and agglomeration literature has emphasized. The clusters often lack interconnected companies and associated institutions. The Korean initiatives provide the hardware, but the software to run the system is missing. Nor have there been coherent visions on what the software should be.[12] Second, the notion of growing world-class individual firms, instead of a network of firms with collaboration among them, has continued to prevail in Korea's quest for an innovation economy. Thus, innovation clusters in the Korean context are about competition to be the chosen one as opposed to generating inter-firm cooperation and spillover effects. In what follows, I will discuss the Taiwanese experience so as to substantiate my argument with an alternative view of SME-based innovation and network relations.

The quest for innovation and export diversification: Taiwan as a comparison case[13]

The distinctive feature of Taiwan's post-war export-led development is decentralized industrialization: First, the SME-based production system encompasses an extensive division of labor, in which firms complement each other in the production process. They cluster in geographical locales. Extensive subcontracting is also exercised within the parts sector. The various components within a part are subcontracted to small factories that specialize in manufacturing that particular part. Second, the SME production network consists of numerous independent parts makers and processing specialists that focus on intermediate inputs and do not make the final product. Third, production networks are decentralized, in that they are open and non-dependent networks in which suppliers and specialist firms are usually not tied to particular assemblers or suppliers; they can supply to several firms within the industry or sell to other industries. Lastly, what distinguishes Taiwan's SMEs from their counterparts in other countries, such as Japan, the United States, France, and Korea (see Chapter 4), is that

Taiwan's SMEs are in charge of export activities. In particular, parts makers and specialist firms actively participate in the global production network as independent specialist subcontractors and compete directly in the world market, rather than being completely dependent on domestic assemblers.

One direct consequence of such decentralized industrialization is that inter-industry linkages are high. The ability of the Taiwanese parts makers to engage directly in the export market and connect to different production networks means having access to novel information flows by connecting to different clusters. An immediate outcome of the free flow of information among industries permits the parts sector to pursue improvement and innovations at the intermediate input level, which can be applied to many situations, instead of at the stage of the end product. In turn, cross-industry learning often leads to adaptation of new materials and new manufacturing technologies through recombination of ideas. Therefore, cross-industry linkages and the organizational principles of the SME network production system provide a strong basis of learning and innovation in Taiwanese SMEs' transition to higher value-added production.

While the dominant understanding of Taiwan's industrial ascent has focused on the success of the information technology sector (IT), various industries in Taiwan's machinery sector, mostly SMEs, have also continued to move up the value chain and be strong exporters in the global market. Clusters continued to thrive in Taiwan in addition to internationalization of production, contrary to the predicted "hollowing out" of SME-based industries (Hsieh 2014). In what follows, I will present examples of how the SME-network system has continued to have an impact on the state-industry linkages in Taiwan's quest for innovation. The rise of Taiwan's metal and machinery sector involves an unacknowledged but widely practiced model of loosely coupled Taiwanese para-state agencies coordinating with a series of SMEs to establish the quality and technical capacities needed to succeed in the global market. Attention is focused on the para-state institutions that serve as the institutionalized linkages between the state and the system of SMEs, including various industry-specific R&D centers and the Metal Industries Research Development Center (MIRDC).

To start: Industry-specific R&D centers that work with the parts sector have been crucial in sustaining the technological capabilities of these parts makers. Having access to industry-specific R&D centers in Taiwan means that SMEs, especially parts makers, can tap into the external economies provided by these public research agencies in areas where an individual SME is unlikely to be able to function effectively on its own. Instead of focusing on capability building of individual SMEs, these collective problem-solving services, such as testing and standards compliance, alleviate the burdens of SMEs by reducing entry barriers for export and R&D. For instance, industry-specific R&D centers have been instrumental in building internationally accredited testing facilities in the machinery sector. In the case of the auto-parts industry, to be accepted as AM suppliers, they need to pass the testing requirement for entering the EU and US markets. In other cases, changes in EU regulations and EU industrial standards have affected the manufacturing methods of machine tools and components.

Yet an individual SME is not likely to meet these requirements on its own. The supporting industry R&D centers disseminate information on changing regulations in the export markets and the respective implications for changes in manufacturing and possible solutions. Moreover, testing facilities have been important for product development for SMEs and for troubleshooting (Interviews ARTC2013; PMC 2011; MIRDC 2013; MPF 2013; BRL 2011). The result is export diversification by SMEs in the machinery and transportation sectors. For instance, in the past decade, about half the total exports went to the top five destinations in the aggregated transportation industries, while over one-third of the total exports went to destinations outside the top 10 countries. In the machinery sector, over 50 percent of the total export value went to countries outside the top 10 export destinations, while the top five export destinations received less than 50 percent of the total exports (Hsieh 2014).

These public institutions are crucial for sustaining SME production networks. They coordinate the decentralized networks by developing the supply chains and matching different production networks. Their technology extension services focus on the development aspect of R&D: enhancing local spillover effects, integration, and developing technical capabilities of the entire supply chain as opposed to growing the capabilities of individual firms or transferring crucial technology to individual chosen firms, as discussed in the Korean experience. For instance, Taiwan used to be the number one exporter of fasteners, with SME-based industry clustered in southern Taiwan. Despite losing advantages to other lower wage countries, the cluster has survived and many companies have moved from low-end standardized fasteners for construction to a higher grade for auto parts suppliers and the aerospace industry. The transition involves working with the whole supply chain for fasteners and tapping into the decentralized network for collective upgrading. The MIRDC was crucial in coordinating the upgrading process by introducing new technologies and working with machine tool firms and the fastener parts makers to develop the required equipment for the new precision manufacturing technology. In turn, the technology could be widely extended as the equipment can be built domestically. The upgrading has cascaded not just within the fastener manufacturers but to a wide range of auxiliary specialists and equipment manufacturers (Hsieh 2014).

Public technology support agencies also play an orchestrating role in bridging different networks and resources. In the context of a decentralized industrial structure, technology adaptation and breakthroughs often occur at the level of intermediate input (meaning the parts sector) and work upward and downward along the supply chain to create backward linkages. Here, the public technology support agencies connect SMEs from different production networks and facilitate the cross-industry fertilization in which innovations and breakthroughs occur through recombination of existing means. This is in direct contrast to the Korean experience where the state connects varieties of agencies and resources to individual firms. For instance, with the emergence of electronic applications on auto components, an increasing number of IT component makers are entering the field of automobile components by collaborating with auto parts makers.

Here, the Automotive Industry Research and Testing Center (ARTC) connected firms in the IT industry with auto parts component makers to pursue and orchestrate the development of such applications (Interview ARTC 2013).

In short, these initiatives, while not consuming large R&D expenditures, have been successful in sustaining clusters, building technological capacities, alleviating SMEs' R&D burden, and averting risks. As the Taiwan experience illustrates, public support institutions are connected to the decentralized industrial system by addressing collective needs and helping parts makers insert themselves into global production networks and succeed in the global market. This includes efforts to sustain networks that are neither conventionally acknowledged nor understood: encouraging skill formation; introducing new manufacturing technologies and disseminating information, thus lowering the entry barriers for SMEs; and matching different production chains for recombining ideas to construct cross-sectoral ties. These partnerships between the lower-rank R&D centers and SMEs affect the subsequent form of technological learning in the SMEs where each actor (including state agencies) is connected in multiple directions. There, the actors' concerns have been to develop industries that will tap into external economies, as opposed to facilitating growth of individual firms. By not picking winners, these initiatives have preserved horizontal inter-firm collaborations, encouraged inter-sector exchange, and recombined resources among different networks, which is conducive to innovation and technology diffusion, as can be seen in the industrial upgrading experience of the machinery sector.

Conclusions

The comparison between the Korean and Taiwanese experiences demonstrates two approaches to industrial transformation with completely different notions of clustering and ways of constructing cross-cutting ties in facilitating innovation. Despite emphasis on demand-responsive policies with numerous nationally devised regional clustering initiatives in Korea, the empirical case studies presented suggest a firm-growth approach has continued to prevail by connecting individual firms to varieties of support agencies so that they will grow and compete globally. The incentive instrument has continued to rely on financial subsidies to individual chosen firms (in the form of R&D subsidies and grants) to promote R&D activities. Korean state-led decentralized innovation policies, rather than breeding entrepreneurships and the diffusion of ideas, generate bureaucratic sprawl and intensify competition among firms. This winner-picking approach to clustering actually undermines potential collaboration and networking among firms, contrary to the expectations of theorists and practitioners regarding such clusters. Learning remains inside the firms. This finding reaffirms the argument that characterizes Korea's high technology development as development without inter-firm networking (Sohn and Kenney 2007).

On the other hand, the Taiwanese case demonstrates more horizontal and decentralized connections among firms and between firms and public research institutes, where each actor is connected in multiple directions. Learning takes place not only within the firm but also by working with other networks of firms. The lessons that can be learned from the Taiwanese SMEs call attention to an alternative path to network-based innovation for latecomers. The specific ways in which the Taiwanese state has connected with the decentralized industrial system have helped to preserve horizontal collaboration among firms and to form a broad-based entrepreneurship in the upgrading quest. This was done through varieties of lower-ranked industrial R&D centers and public research institutes that build external economies, solve collective problems, and extend technology to develop local supply chains to ensure cross-industry spillover effects.

In line with the analysis, my hunch is that the Korean model will grow individual leading national and global champions, whereas the Taiwanese path will grow groups of hidden champions that complement each other in climbing up the global value chains. To succeed in the next stage of the innovation quest, the question that concerns the Korean model will continue to be how to identify best-practice SMEs and an ecosystem that could nurture individual promising actors regardless of the national or regional support systems. The question that dominates the Taiwanese model will continue to be how to sustain the territorial-rooted clusters and nourish a system that comprises a network of firms complementing each other and tapping into external economies in the face of internationalization.

Notes

1 For a review of the old industrial complex/cluster program, see Lee (2001).
2 The MOCIE (Ministry of Commerce, Industry, and Energy) was responsible for regional innovation initiatives during Roh's administration. Subsequently, a large part of MOCIE became the Ministry of Knowledge Economy (MKE) during Lee's administration (2008–2013).
3 A mini-cluster is the industry-academia-research labs alliance composed according to an industry/technical field that aims to develop mutual cooperation, joint-learning, and sharing of information continuously among innovative agents in the region, including companies (both large firms and SMEs, universities, research institutes, and support institutions) (MKE and KICOX 2011, 12).
4 For detailed information on the goals of GSTEP, see the organization's website at www.gstep.re.kr/eng/html/research/gstep_business_02.asp.
5 Pangyo Techno Valley claims to have become Korea's Silicon Valley, aiming to attract global companies and local innovative companies in IT and biotech industries and to encourage start-ups. GSTEP oversees the project. See the Pangyo website for further details: www.pangyotechnovalley.org/eng/html/introduce/index.asp.
6 Kim Young-won, "Shaping Korean start-up scene: Gyeonggi science technology center serves as bridge between start-ups and tech heavyweights," *The Korean Herald*, April 7, 2016, www.koreaherald.com/view.php?ud=20160407000692. Accessed October 14, 2016.
7 Simon Mundy, "South Korea aims for creative economy to end reliance on *chaebol*: Government rolls out funding and infrastructure to aid start-ups and revitalize SME sector," *Financial Times*, June 24, 2015, www.ft.com/content/9203e38c-0dab-11e5-9a65-00144feabdc0. Accessed April 6, 2016.

8 Huh Sung-soo, "Creative Economy: New Paradigm of Economic Policy Creates Visible Results Centered on Creative Innovation Centers," *Business Korea*, May 3, 2016, www.businesskorea.co.kr/english/features/cover-stories/14582-creative-economy-new-paradigm-economic-policy-creates-visible-results. Accessed October 12, 2016.

9 A total of 18 creative economy and innovation centers (창조경제혁신센터) were created in which central and local governments work in conjunction with *chaebols* to create an ecosystem to nurture and support the expansion of SMEs across regions, with particular emphasis on start-ups. Each *chaebol* is assigned to an innovation center according to its expertise. For a brief summary of the program, see Choi Yang-hee, "Creative Economy: springboard for Korea's leap forward," *Korea Times*, September 29, 2015, www.koreatimes.co.kr/www/news/biz/2015/09/123_187696.html. Accessed April 6, 2016.

10 Lee Song-hoon, "Driving Creative Economy: KICOX Pledges to Make Korean Industry Base of Creative Economy," *Business Korea*, January 6, 2016, www.business korea.co.kr/english/news/industry/13473-driving-creative-economy-kicox-pledges-make-korean-industry-base-creative. Accessed October 13, 2016.

11 The news was posted by one of the companies selected in 2014, Dunhwa Entec Co., a manufacturer of heat-exchanger for the marine, petro-chemical, and power generation industry, as an indication for their technology prowess. www.dh.co.kr/English/pr/news01.asp?act=view&encData=skey%E3%80%8D%E3%80%8Csstr%E3%80%8D%E3%80%8Ccate%E3%80%8D%E3%80%8Cpage%E3%80%8D1%E3%80%8Cidx%E3%80%8D3689.

12 The question of what the software should be is often raised in the agency's self-evaluation. See Yim et al. (2010).

13 The following section develops from Hsieh (2014).

References

Amsden, Alice H. 1989. Asia's next giant: South Korea and late industrialization. New York: Oxford University Press.

Amsden, Alice H., and Wan-Wen Chu. 2003. Beyond Late Development: Taiwan's Upgrading Policies. Cambridge: MIT Press.

Block, Fred, and Matthew R. Keller., eds. 2011. State of Innovation: The U.S. Government's Role in Technology Development. Boulder: Paradigm Publishers.

Block, Fred. 2008. "Swimming Against the Current: The Rise of a Hidden Developmental State in the United States." Politics & Society 36 (2):169–206.

Castilla, Emilio J., Hokyu Hwang, Ellen Granovetter, and Mark Granovetter. 2000. "Social Networks in Silicon Valley." In The Silicon Valley Edge: A Habitat for Innovation and Entrepreneurship, eds. Chong-Moon Lee, William Miller, Marguerite Hancock and Henry Rowen. Stanford: Stanford University Press, 218–247.

Choi, Yang-hee. 2015. "Creative economy: Springboard for Korea's leap forward." The Korea Times, September 29, 2015. www.koreatimes.co.kr/www/news/biz/2015/09/123_187696.html.

Chung, Sunyang. 1999. "Korean innovation policies for small and medium-sized enterprises." Science and Public Policy 26 (2):70–82.

Evans, Peter B. 1995. Embedded autonomy: states and industrial transformation. Princeton, NJ: Princeton University Press.

Hassink, Robert. 2001. "Towards regionally embedded innovation support systems in South Korea? Case studies from Kyongbuk-Taegu and Kyonggi." Urban Studies 38 (8):1373–1395.

Hassink, Robert. 2004. "Regional Innovation Support Systems in South Korea and Germany Compared." Erdkunde 58 (2): 156–171.

Herrigel, Gary. 1996. Industrial Constructions: The Sources of German Industrial Power. Cambridge: Cambridge University Press.

Hsieh, Michelle F. 2011. "Similar opportunities, different responses: Explaining the divergent patterns of development between Taiwan and South Korea." International Sociology 26 (3): 364–391.

Hsieh, Michelle F. 2014. "Hollowing Out or Sustaining? Taiwan's SME Network-based Production System Reconsidered." Taiwanese Sociology (28): 149–191.

Huh, Sung-soo. 2016. "Creative Economy: New Paradigm of Economic Policy Creates Visible Results Centered on Creative Innovation Centers." Business Korea, May 3, 2016. www.businesskorea.co.kr/english/features/cover-stories/14582-creative-economy-new-paradigm-economic-policy-creates-visible-results.

Kim, Hyung-Joo, Yong-Sook Lee, and Hye-Ran Hwang. 2014. "Regionalization of planned S&T parks: the case of Daedeok S&T Park in Daejeon, South Korea." Environment and Planning C: Government and Policy 32 (5): 843–862.

Kim, Young-won. 2016. "[Herald Interview] Shaping Korean start-up scene: Gyeonggi science technology center serves as bridge between start-ups and tech heavyweights." The Korea Herald, April 7, 2016. www.koreaherald.com/view.php?ud=20160407 000692.

Lazerson, Mark. 1995. "A New Phoenix?: Modern Putting-Out in the Modena Knitwear Industry." Administrative Science Quarterly 40 (1): 34–59.

Lee, Kong-Rae. 2001. "From fragmentation to integration: development process of innovation clusters in Korea." Science Technology & Society, 6(2): 305–327.

Lee, Song-hoon. 2016. "Driving Creative Economy: KICOX Pledges to Make Korean Industry Base of Creative Economy." Business Korea, January 6, 2016. www.businesskorea.co.kr/english/news/industry/13473-driving-creative-economy-kicox-pledges-make-korean-industry-base-creative.

Lee, Yong-Sook. 2009. "Balanced Development in Globalizing Regional Development? Unpacking the New Regional Policy of South Korea." Regional Studies 43 (3): 353–367.

Lee, Yong-Sook. 2012. "Clusters as a policy panacea? Critical reflections on the cluster policies of South Korea." In Locating Neoliberalism in East Asia: Neoliberalizing Spaces in Developmental States: 148–166.

Lim, Haeran. 1998. Korea's Growth and Industrial Transformation. New York: St. Martin's Press.

MKE (Ministry of Knowledge Economy), and KICOX. 2011. The Industrial Complex Cluster Program of Korea. Korea Industrial Complex Corporation.

Mundy, Simon. 2015. "South Korea aims for creative economy to end reliance on *chaebol*: Government rolls out funding and infrastructure to aid start-ups and revitalize SME sector." Financial Times, June 24, 2015. www.ft.com/content/9203e38c-0dab-11e5-9a65-00144feabdc0.

Negoita, Marian, and Fred Block. 2012. "Networks and Public Policies in the Global South: The Chilean Case and the Future of the Developmental Network State." Studies in Comparative International Development (SCID): 1–22.

Ó Riain, Seán. 2004. The Politics of High Tech Growth: Developmental Network States in the global economy. Cambridge: Cambridge University Press.

Park, Sam Ock, and Yangmi Koo. 2013. "Innovation-driven cluster development strategies in Korea." European Review of Industrial Economics and Policy 5.

Piore, Michael J., and Charles F. Sabel. 1984. The Second Industrial Divide: Possibilities for Prosperity. New York: Basic Books.

Powell, Walter W. 1990. "Neither Market nor Hierarchy: Networks Forms of Organization." Research in Organizational Behavior 12 (2): 295–336.

Powell, Walter W., Kenneth W. Koput, and Laurel Smith-Doerr. 1996. "Interorganizational collaboration and the locus of innovation: Networks of learning in biotechnology." Administrative Science Quarterly 41 (1): 116–145.

Sakakibara, Mariko, and Dong-Sung Cho. 2002. "Cooperative R&D in Japan and Korea: a comparison of industrial policy." Research Policy 31 (5): 673–692.

Saxenian, AnnaLee. 1994. Regional Advantage: Culture and Competition in Silicon Valley and Route 128. Cambridge: Harvard University Press.

Saxenian, AnnaLee, and Jinn-Yuh Hsu. 2001. "The Silicon Valley-Hsinchu connection: technical communities and industrial upgrading." Industrial and Corporate Change 10 (4): 893–920.

Smith-Doerr, Laurel, and Walter W. Powell. 2005. "Networks and Economic Life." In The Handbook of Economic Sociology, eds. Neil Smelser and Richard Swedberg, 379–402. Princeton: Princeton University Press.

Sohn, Dong-Won, and Martin Kenney. 2007. "Universities, clusters, and innovation systems: The case of Seoul, Korea." World Development 35 (6): 991–1004.

Weiss, Linda. 1998. The Myth of the Powerless State. Ithaca: Cornell University Press.

Yim, Deok Soon, Jong Bin Im, Jung Seok Kim, and Soo Jin Kim. 2010. "Evaluation of Gwanggyo Techno valley in Korea and policy implication for the regional innovation." Technology Management for Global Economic Growth (PICMET). IEEE: 1–7.

6 College major and female labor supply

Jihye Kam and Soohyung Lee

There is little doubt that the male-centric nature of Korean society and corporate culture contributes to the strategic and operational shortcomings of the *chaebol* and SMEs alike, as described by the first five chapters of this volume. A male-centric culture is deeply rooted in Korean society, as shown by various measures such as the sex ratio imbalance at birth through the 1990s, rigid gender roles, and low female representation in leadership positions. According to World Values Survey data, from 2010 to 2014, 54.1 percent of Koreans agreed that "when jobs are scarce, men should have more right to a job than women," compared with 7.6 percent of Americans.[1] In regard to leadership positions, 41.3 percent of Koreans agreed that "on the whole, men make better business executives than woman do," compared with 11.6 percent of Americans.[2] This perception of gender roles might be reflected in the low percentage of females in leadership positions. For example, only 13 out of 1,787 firms listed on the Korean stock exchange have female CEOs (0.7 percent, CEO Score 2013). Relatedly, only 15.7 percent of parliamentarians are female, placing Korea the sixth lowest among OECD countries (OECD 2013).[3]

Although there is evidence that such gender stereotypes are receding in the Korean mindset (see Chapter 1), they continue to be major obstacles for women to remain in the workplace, let alone rise up the professional ladder.[4] In Korea, the female labor market participation rate was only 55.6 percent in 2013, making it one of the bottom five OECD countries (OECD 2016). As described in Panel A of Figure 6.1, the female labor market participation rate in Korea has increased over the past years, except for 1998, when the Asian financial crisis hit the economy, and 2008, when the 2008 economic downturn starting in the USA affected the economic conditions. Korea, however, still shows a sizable deficit of female labor market participants relative to other OECD countries. In Panel B of Figure 6.1, we plot the fraction of female employees among the working-age female population, as an alternative measure of female representation in the labor market, which shows a consistently lower level than the OECD average between 1990 and 2013. Furthermore, Korea was ranked the worst among OECD countries in 2015 in terms of the glass-ceiling index for women and work (see *The Economist* 2016). The under-representation of women in the labor force is concerning particularly because women's educational attainment had

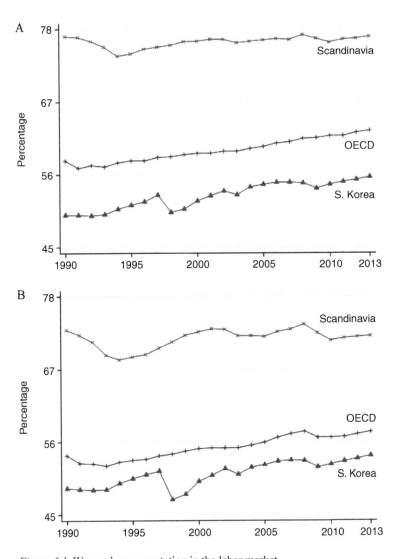

Figure 6.1 Women's representation in the labor market.

substantially increased over the same time period, which should have improved their labor market outcomes (see OECD 2012, 2016a).[5]

The low utilization of the female workforce poses social and economic problems for several reasons. As reviewed in Chapter 1 in this volume, mixed-gender workgroups tend to be more creative and take better risks, and tend to perform better in general than all-male workgroups. For *chaebol* affiliates and SMEs seeking to increase their innovative capabilities—something that Chapters 2, 3, and 5 identified as a pressing need—moving away from homogeneous, male-centric corporate cultures towards a more gender-inclusive culture, has the potential to yield substantial dividends. Even without considering potential benefits to innovation and economic performance, the low utilization of the female workforce becomes salient given the pressure of population aging (see Chapter 1 for an overview). One concern regarding population aging is the possibility that each worker may need to take on a greater economic burden to support a larger number of elderly retired people, for example by paying more for social security and healthcare. In this regard, a low female representation in the workforce might be associated with even greater economic burden per worker to support retirees. For all of these reasons, the large gender disparity in labor market outcomes observed in Korea deserves close attention.

The low female labor market participation rate and employment to population ratio contributed to a pension-age population per 100 employees among the working-age population of 25.9 in 2013, much larger than the age dependence ratio, 16.7. Any increase in female representation may lead to a decrease in the economic burden of population aging in Korea. To get a realistic sense of the possible impact of the increase, we examine two hypothetical situations. One is the situation in which the female employment to population ratio in Korea is increased to the average level of OECD countries.[6] The other is the situation in which the Korean female employment to population ratio increases to match that of Scandinavian countries.[7] We find that the number of pension-age population per 100 working-age employees would decrease by 2.6 or 12.0 percent if the female employment ratio were the same as that of OECD average or the Scandinavian average, respectively.[8]

Whether women's employment level should be increased to address societal concerns in Korea is a question beyond the scope of this chapter.[9] Rather, this chapter takes for granted the need for an increase in women's employment, and it aims to uncover observable factors, particularly college-major choice. The distribution of college major may have been affected by government policies, which could have shaped female labor market outcomes.

College major in addressing labor market gender disparity

This chapter focuses on college-major choice as a factor that may contribute to the low level of female employment and that also may be used as a policy tool for the following reasons. The gender gap in overall educational attainment is no longer sufficient to explain the gender gap in labor market outcomes. For example, as shown in Figure 6.2, the percentage of female high school graduates enrolled in a tertiary educational institution has dramatically increased (line with triangles).[10] The female enrollment rate for two-year colleges has exceeded that for males by 1990 (line with crosses), and even if we focus on the enrollment rate of four-year colleges, the female enrollment rate outnumbered that males in 2007 (line with x's). Therefore, educational attainment per se cannot account for the low female representation in the labor market.

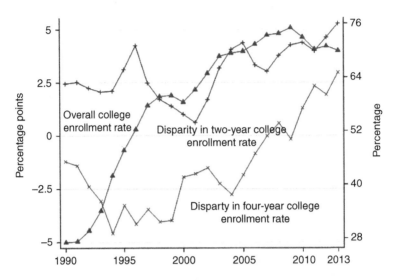

Figure 6.2 College enrollment.

Despite gender parity in overall educational attainment, men and women show stark differences in terms of what fields they major in (herein, college major). While men are more likely to major in Engineering, which offers good career prospects, women are more likely to select Humanities and Arts/Athletics majors, which offer poor career prospects. Therefore, nudging women into the Engineering major might improve their labor market outcomes in terms of employment, earnings, and the security of job tenure. Better labor market outcomes can contribute to stronger labor market participation by females, and consequently enlarge the economic capacity of Korea to cope with its rising dependency ratio. To encourage women to major in Engineering, various methods could be employed, such as providing more accurate information of job prospects, campaigning female empowerment in STEM fields, or implementing policies on gender-conscious affirmative action in college admissions. This chapter focuses on the possibility of nudging women into Engineering majors, which are regarded as predominantly male disciplines, through gender-neutral policy implementation by analyzing micro-data of college graduates.

Before we present our analysis, it is worth noting that designing a policy tool to directly affect individuals' college-major choices might be infeasible in general settings. However, in Korea, it could be a reasonable policy tool because the Ministry of Education (MOE) has substantial influence over both public and private four-year colleges because of their heavy dependence of budget on tuition fees and government transfers. For example, on average, 53.8 percent of the budget of public four-year colleges was funded through government transfers in 2009. As for private four-year colleges, on average, tuition fees account for over 65.4 percent of their financing in Korea, over twice that of the US's reliance on tuition fees (33.3 percent in 2009) (see details in Korean Educational Development Institute 2012). The MOE's controls on both tuition rates and government transfers to colleges, enables the MOE to greatly affect the decision of a college, ultimately influencing an individual's college-major choice.

In addition to governing tuition rates and government transfers to colleges, the MOE has regulated the maximum number of incoming freshman seats in each college but never issued explicit interventions on the number of seats for each major within a college. Accordingly, each college in theory can freely distribute its allowed seats across its majors based on its own core mission and values. In practice, however, each college may reduce the size of one major to increase the seats in another major to be aligned with a MOE's policy guideline and obtain funding incentives from the MOE.

A representative example showing the MOE's influence over college-major quotas is the "PRIME project, which is the largest and most controversial, government subsidy program in higher education." The policy provides monetary incentives and priority in receiving government resources to universities if they reallocate major quotas to Engineering majors.[11] This policy was announced in 2015, effective as of the 2017 admission cycle. If selected as a PRIME project participating institution, each college will be funded on average 9.3 billion won per year.[12] Seventy-five colleges submitted a proposal describing their tactical plan for reallocation of seats in favor of Engineering major through this program. In May 2016, the MOE chose 21 colleges for the PRIME project based on the effectiveness and feasibility of a strategy for restructuring academic programs. Starting with the 2017 admission cohort, financially supported for three years by the MOE, the 21 colleges have began to reallocate approximately 10 percent of their seats to the Engineering major, while reducing seats in Humanities, Social Science, Natural Sciences/Mathematics, and Arts/Athletics majors.[13] Even colleges that were not part of the PRIME project designed upcoming college admission quotas in line with those of these 21 colleges for the possibility of participating in the PRIME or other relevant projects in the future.[14] Although the PRIME project is a gender-neutral policy, it may lead to the reallocation of females to Engineering majors from other majors because of gender differences in responsiveness to education policy changes. We will discuss it later along with explaining the possibility of policy interventions on a nudge of women into Engineering majors. Thus, these institutional features in Korea make it possible to alter individuals' choices of college major, particularly for women, by changing the supply of college majors.

College majors and labor market outcomes

To examine our conjecture, we use the Graduates Occupational Mobility Survey (GOMS), a nationally representative survey of young adults in Korea who graduated from either a two-year or four-year college. The GOMS surveys demographic information on individuals and their labor market outcomes 20 months after college graduation.[15] We use all eight waves of GOMS between 2005 and 2013 and construct a sample consisting of four-year college graduates.

We narrow our sample to only four-year college graduates because two-year colleges are vocational schools typically tied to certain firms where they send their graduates to work, and vocational and four-year colleges are not comparable with each other even if they offer the same majors.

We classify college majors into seven groups: Engineering, Humanities, Social Science, Education, Natural Science/Mathematics, Medicine/Public Health, and Arts/Athletics.[16] We examine the performance of each college major relative to Engineering with respect to three outcomes: the share of graduates who are employed, the share of graduates who hold a long-term job position among those employed, and the average monthly earnings. Note that we do not report our findings with respect to a college graduate's labor market participation status because there is little variation across college majors and gender. The limited variation is expected because, in our data, most individuals are never married and have no children, and thus are likely to look for a job.

To evaluate labor market performance across college majors, we take the average of each labor market outcome for a given college major. These major-specific mean-level outcomes are compared by calculating the difference between a given major and Engineering, divided by the average of an Engineering major. The latter division expresses the gap in the same unit across all three variables. Figure 6.3 reports the results across genders, while Figure 6.4 reports the patterns by gender. In these figures, a negative bar indicates that, on average, the corresponding college major shows lower performance relative to the Engineering major. For example, the first three bars from the left in Figure 6.3 show that, on average, college graduates majoring in Humanities are 7.6 percent less likely to be

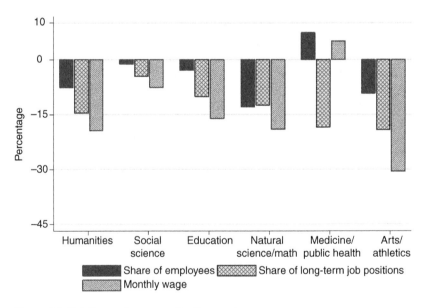

Figure 6.3 Relative performance of college majors.

employed, 14.6 percent less likely to hold a long-term job position conditional on being employed, and earn a 19.5 percent lower monthly wage. Figure 6.3 shows that except for Medicine and Public Health, on average, college graduates with Engineering degrees outperform those with other degrees with respect to job finding, job quality, and earnings. These findings qualitatively remain the same when we conduct the analysis by gender (see Figure 6.4. Panels A and B).[17]

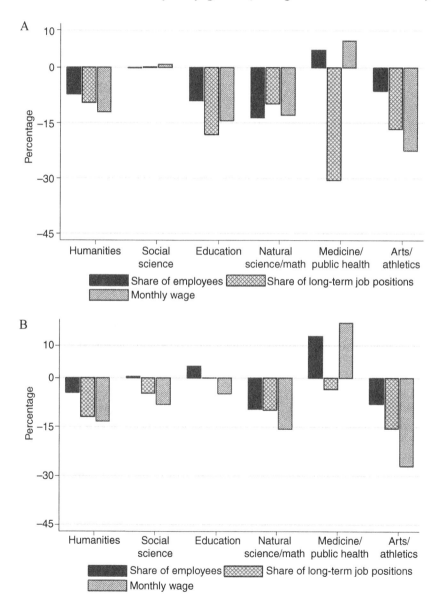

Figure 6.4 Relative performance of college majors by gender.

Furthermore, the outperformance of Engineering graduates qualitatively remains the same even when we use regression models to control for other observable characteristics such as age, location, and survey year (see Cho et al. 2016 for details).

Gender disparity in college major distribution: status and labor market implications

Although substantial differences in employment and earnings exist across college majors in Korea, women are more likely than men to choose college majors that are disadvantageous in terms of labor market outcomes.[18] Figure 6.5 shows the distribution of college majors by gender. In our sample, 31.8 percent of female college graduates major in Humanities or Arts/Athletics, the two majors exhibiting the lowest labor market performance, while only 10.3 percent major in Engineering. In contrast, only 16.1 percent of male college graduates choose Humanities or Arts/Athletics, while 38.8 percent major in Engineering.

This gender disparity in college major distribution accounts for a substantial part of the gender gap in labor market outcomes. We estimate the extent to which being female is associated with negative labor market outcomes with and without controlling for college majors. Suppose that the difference in college-major choices entirely accounts for the gender gap in labor market outcomes. Then, once we control for college majors, whether a person is female or not would have no explanatory power on the person's labor market outcomes. Therefore, the difference in estimates with and without controlling for college majors informs us about the extent to which college major may account for gender gap in the labor market outcomes.

Following this idea, using Logit models, we estimate the impact of college major on labor market outcomes such as the likelihood of being employed and having a long-term job position.[19] In addition, we analyze a person's logarithm of monthly earnings using a linear regression model similar to the Mincerian regression model (Mincer 1974).[20] In our regression analyses, we additionally include dummies for college entrance years, survey years, and residence fixed effects to capture potential difference across cohorts, survey years, and locations. To examine the extent to which college major may account for the gender gap in labor market outcomes, we compare the coefficients of "female" across regressions without and with controlling for college major dummies. Without controlling for college majors, females are on average 1.6 percentage points less likely to be employed, 6.3 percentage points less likely to hold a long-term job position conditional on being employed, and have a 21.5 percent lower monthly wage. The coefficients of female, however, are reduced by 18.1 to 62.5 percent when controlling for college major dummies. Therefore, our findings suggest that college major can account for a substantial part of the gender gap in labor market outcomes (see Table 6.1).

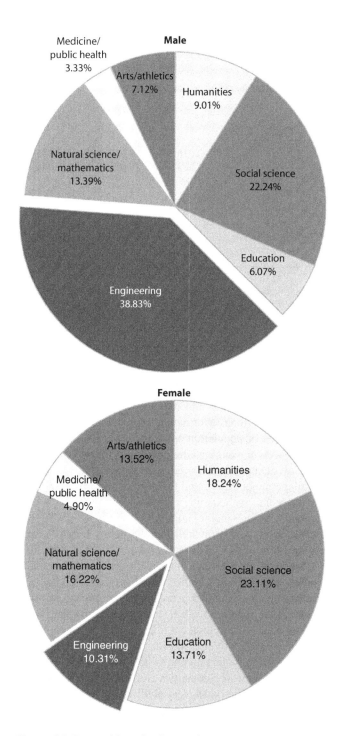

Figure 6.5 Composition of college majors by gender.

Table 6.1 College major and gender gap in labor market outcomes

Outcome	1: employed	1: regular workers	Log monthly earnings
Sample	All (1)	Employees (2)	Employees (3)
Without controlling for college majors (a) Female	−0.016*** (0.003)	−0.063*** (0.003)	−0.215*** (0.004)
With controlling for college majors (b) Female	−0.006* (0.003)	−0.039*** (0.003)	−0.176*** (0.004)
Roll of college majors: (a-b)/(a)	62.50%	38.10%	18.14%
No. of observations	91,344	66,194	65,542

Notes
Columns (1) and (2) – Logit model, marginal effects reported. Column (3) – OLS. Dummies for college entrance years, survey years, and residence fixed effects are included. The standard errors are in parentheses. The asterisks *, **, and *** indicate statistical significance at the 10%, 5%, and 1% levels, respectively.

Possibility of policy interventions and expected effects

The empirical patterns of college-major choices and labor market outcomes suggest that policies nudging women into majors with good career prospects, namely Engineering, may help their labor market representation and their status, easing the economic burden of population aging that each working-age Korean may need to bear. This section examines that possibility in two steps. First, we calculate the extent of economic empowerment Korea may experience by nudging women's college-major choice and the resultant improved labor market outcomes of women. Second, we examine the possibility that educational policies may nudge women's college-major choices.

In the first step, we examine two hypothetical scenarios in which women's choice of college major may differ from the current status. For simplicity, we assume that men's choice of college major remains the same as the actual across both scenarios. Suppose that women's choice of college-major choice were the same as men's in our sample (e.g., a 28.5 percentage point increase in the share of Engineering majors among women). Then, the estimated results reported in Table 6.1 suggest that the female employment to population ratio would increase by 1.1 percentage points. Alternatively, consider a rather modest scenario in which the share of Engineering majors among women was increased by 10 percentage points, while enrollment in Humanities and Arts/Athletics was reduced by 5 percentage points each. This change is predicted to increase the female employment to population ratio by 0.6 percentage points.

Although these predicted impacts may look small in magnitude, they are not small in an economic sense. This is because in Korea, the female employment to population ratio grew by 0.4 percent per year over the past 15 years. Therefore, even the 0.6 percentage point increase predicted under the modest scenario implies that the change in college major shares among women may be able to increase the growth rate of the female employment ratio by a factor of two.

The second step is more challenging because there exists only limited knowledge of what induces a person's choice of college major. In addition to the labor market aspects associated with college major, individuals may make their college-major choice based on various factors, such as their intellectual interests, the information they have about the majors (even if it is not accurate), and the college-major quota available at the time of application. Unfortunately, similar to other countries, information on what guides the college major decision process in Korea is extremely limited.[21] Given this limitation, we neither contemplate all possible policy tools that may affect individuals' college-major choice, nor precisely calculate the expected impact of a policy tool. Rather, we examine one potential policy tool, namely the quota allocation across college majors, and its expected impact on college-major choice and resulting labor market outcomes.

As explained earlier, the Ministry of Education (MOE) in Korea can and has been exercising its influence in setting college-major quotas across all colleges. Therefore, if there were an excess demand for four-year colleges in Korea compared with the total number of seats permitted by the MOE, it is likely that an MOE policy altering the college-major quotas would lead to altering the individuals' choice of college majors. Indeed, for the cohorts who applied to four-year colleges from 2003 to 2015, the average number of individuals who took college entrance tests (CSAT) is over twice as large as the total number of incoming freshman seats in all four-year colleges, suggesting an excess demand for admission to four-year colleges in Korea.[22]

To support our argument, we compare the changes in college-major quota with those of the actual enrollment of students. Given our focus on Engineering majors, we report the patterns with respect to the share of Engineering in three admission cycles—2002, 2007, and 2013. We chose those three years because in the period from 2002 to 2007 the Engineering quota was reduced, while from 2007 to 2013 the quota was increased. The first row of Table 6.2 shows that in the 2002 admission cycle, 27.8 percent of seats (quota) were allocated to the Engineering major,

Table 6.2 College-major quota and enrollment—engineering majors (unit: %)

	2002	2007	2013
Share out of total number of seats	27.82	22.86	24.54
Share out of freshmen	27.27	23.14	24.81
Composition			
Share out of male freshmen	39.96	34.89	36.79
Share out of female freshmen	12.46	9.50	11.21

Source: Statistical yearbook of education, Korean Educational Development Institute and Ministry of Education.

this share was reduced to 22.9 percent by the 2007 admission cycle, but increased back to 24.5 percent in the 2013 admission cycle. Over the same period, the share of freshmen majoring in Engineering was 27.3 percent, 23.1 percent, and 24.8 percent, respectively (the second row of Table 6.2). Although the two series are not exactly the same, the difference is negligible, implying that the college-major quota constrains individuals' college-major choice.[23]

The last two rows in Table 6.2 show that when the Engineering quota fluctuated, the share of female freshmen majoring in Engineering also fluctuated. When the share of Engineering majors was reduced by 5.0 percentage points (2002–2007), the share of female freshmen majoring in Engineering was reduced by 3.0 percentage points. When the share of Engineering majors was increased by 1.7 percentage points (2007–2013), the share of female freshmen majoring in Engineering also increased by 1.7 percentage points. These patterns show that the actual enrollment behavior among women responds to the college-major quotas, suggesting that college-major quota policy may be able to affect female college-major choice and, ultimately, women's labor market outcomes.

Conclusions

Many developed countries face population aging, which requires better mobilization of available labor resources to support the elderly and maintain economic vibrancy and growth. In the context of Korea, this chapter documents the under-utilization of women in the labor market and examines the possibility of better utilization through narrowing the gender gap in college-major choice. We conduct a thought experiment investigating hypothetical scenarios where Korean women were more likely to participate in the workforce because they were more likely to study in fields offering good career prospects. Using a nationally representative dataset of recent college graduates, we find that while men are more likely to major in Engineering, which offers good career prospects, women are more likely to select Humanities and Arts/Athletics majors that offer poor career prospects. Therefore, nudging more women into Engineering majors might increase their employment and earnings, and, consequently, enlarge Korea's economic capacity to cope with the increasing elderly population.

In Korea, we find an excess demand for incoming freshman seats at four-year colleges relative to the total number of seats granted, together with regulations on college-major quota across colleges. These institutional features allow for the possibility that a policy increasing the quota of Engineering majors may directly affect individuals' college-major choice.

Our findings may also be useful to other countries that are trying to boost female representation in STEM fields. Even if a government does not explicitly affect the supply of college majors as Korea does, its policy-makers may be able to influence the supply by providing proper incentives. For example, in 2009, the Obama administration introduced the "Educate to Innovate" initiative to promote STEM majors among American students, especially among women and minorities (White House 2013a, 2013b, 2015).

Notes

1 The World Value Survey includes a few other statements about gender roles. Examples include "on the whole, men make better political leaders than women do," "a university education is more important for a boy than for a girl," and "if a woman earns more money than her husband, it's almost certain to cause problems."

2 The fractions are calculated among those who expressed agreement or disagreement, excluding non-respondents and those who reserved their opinion.

3 The percentage represents the number of women parliamentarians as a share of total filled seats, which was recorded as of October 31, 2012.

4 For example, Kim Hyun-kyung, Vice President of Hankook Tire, said that "a deep-rooted attachment to traditional gender roles in Korea remains a big hurdle for working women," and that "the thinking about women's role as a primary caregiver and educator for children is unlikely to change any time soon." Cited in Woo (2013).

5 The OECD (2012) concludes that

> The considerable gains in educational attainment have yet to translate into better labor market outcomes for women; female labor force participation rates are about the same now as 20 years ago (55 percent compared to the OECD average of 65 percent) with 10 percent of all managerial positions being by women (compared to about one-third across the OECD). The gender pay gap is also the highest among OECD countries at 39 percent, but at 10 percent the gap is considerably smaller among young adults.

6 The OECD average is calculated as the mean of the data values for all OECD countries for which data are available.

7 Scandinavian countries include Norway, Sweden, and Denmark, which are well-known for their high levels of female labor market participation. According to the OECD Statistics, the female employment to population ratio in 2013 was 73.5 percent in Norway, 72.5 percent in Sweden, and 70.0 percent in Denmark. The simple average of the three countries is 72.0 percent.

8 Authors' calculations. All data are extracted from the OECD Statistics (Demography and Population: Population Statistics and Labour: Labour Force Statistics).

9 For example, to be in the labor force, women may need to reduce other activities such as time for leisure and household chores. Thus, Korean women may show low labor market participation rate because they value their leisure and utility from household chores much more than working, relative to women in other countries. Alternatively, if the low female labor market participation rate is caused by gender discrimination prevalent in the Korean society, then policies promoting women's presence in the labor force may benefit women.

10 Tertiary educational institutions include four-year universities (herein, colleges), junior colleges, universities of education, four-year military academies, industrial universities, technical colleges, distance/cyber universities, colleges in the company, polytechnic colleges, specialization colleges, and miscellaneous school undergraduates, junior college courses.

11 The official title of the project is the "Program for Industry Needs – Matched Education (PRIME) project." This project, devised in 2015, has been effective since March 2016. The project's objectives are twofold. One objective is to reduce the total quota of a university to address the fact that the school-age population has been shrinking. The other objective is to reduce the relative quota of a major that is not well demanded in the Korean labor market and reallocate that freed quota to another major that is well demanded (e.g., from Humanities to Engineering).

12 If selected as leading colleges for education matched to social demand, colleges would be annually funded 15 billion won. If selected as leading colleges for education

based on creativity, colleges would be annually funded 5 billion won. The MOE plans to spend total 600 billion won for three years.

13 See the Ministry of Education's press release on May 4, 2016.

14 Kang (2016) reported the 2017 college admission plans proposed by the four-year college associations.

15 The GOMS used to survey college graduates 20 months after college graduation and two years after the initial survey. For example, the 2005 GOMS includes individuals who graduated from college in August 2004 or February 2005 and it surveys their initial labor market outcomes in 2006 and then two years later, in 2008. However, the follow-up survey was discontinued in 2011. Thus, we, analyze the pooled sample constructed using data from 2005 to 2013 initial surveys.

16 Medicine/Public Health majors train individuals to be medical doctors, nurses, pharmacists, physiologists, chiropractors, dental hygienists, nutritionists, therapists, and other healthcare providers.

17 For example, consider Humanities. On average, male college graduates majoring in Humanities are 7.34 percent less likely to be employed, 9.60 percent less likely to hold a long-term job position conditional on being employed, and earn a 12.05 percent lower monthly wage. Similarly, female college graduates majoring in Humanities are 4.43 percent less likely to be employed, 11.84 percent less likely to hold a long-term job position conditional on being employed, and earn a 13.17 percent lower monthly wage.

18 Much of literature has attempted to identify the possible reasons accounting for the gender disparity in college-major choice by investigating gender differences in attitudes and preferences (Zafar 2013) and social and environmental factors such as gender stereotyping or discrimination, and rigid gender roles (Tolley 2014).

19 Logit models describe the response probabilities of the dependent variable which is dichotomous or qualitative binary. In the logit model, a logistic link function is applied to transform the predicted values into probabilities.

20 The Mincerian regression model is a benchmark model for the estimation of the pecuniary returns to schooling. The basic form of the Mincerian regression model assumes a linear effect of years of schooling on earnings.

21 For example, individuals may choose their college major based on their abilities, preferences, and career prospects associated with college majors. Information on abilities and preferences, however, is extremely limited in usual survey data. Furthermore, recent studies show that individuals may have insufficient information on college majors and also have biased beliefs about their own expected future earnings and other major-specific aspects were they to major in different majors (e.g., Wiswall and Zafar 2015). The literature developed in economics has just started uncovering these mechanisms but is not yet sufficiently informative about individuals' decision-making mechanisms.

22 For example, the total number of incoming freshman seats of four-year colleges were 332 (1000 seats) in 2003, 332 in 2009, and 335 in 2015, whereas the number of CSAT takers were 655 (1000 persons) in 2003, 559 in 2009, and 595 in 2015 (Korean Educational Development Institute 2016; Korea Institute for Curriculum and Evaluation, 2016).

23 There is a small gap between the college-major quota and the enrollment in Table 6.2. This is because the MOE reports the distribution of college majors among freshmen, including a small number of students who are not subject to the college-major quota. For example, college applicants who are not Korean citizens are not subject to the college-major quota.

References

CEO Score. 2013. "The number of female CEOs at firms listed on the Korean stock exchange is only 13 at 14 firms, which is 0.73 percent." March 8, 2013. Accessed on September 1, 2016. [in Korean] www.ceoscore.co.kr/bbs/board.php?bo_table=S00 L04&wr_id=22&page=8.

Cho, Sungjin, Jihye Kam, and Soohyung Lee. 2018. "Efficient Supply of Human Capital: Role of College Major." Singapore Economic Review 63(1), 1–25.

Kang, Bongjin. 2016. "The number of incoming freshman seats will be decreased by 10 thousands." Maeil Kyungjae News. July 14, 2016. Accessed on August 15, 2016. [in Korean] http://news.mk.co.kr/newsRead.php?sc=30000022&year=2016&no=438955.

Korean Educational Development Institute. 2012. "Statistics Series for Korean and Global Education: College Tuition and Finance." January 2, 2012. Accessed on September 3, 2016. [in Korean] http://cesi.kedi.re.kr/index.

Korean Educational Development Institute. 2016. "Korean Educational Statistics Service." Public-use data file and documentation. Accessed on August 31, 2016. http://cesi.kedi.re.kr/.

Korea Institute for Curriculum and Evaluation. 2016. "Yearly Statistics on College Scholastic Ability Test Takers." Public-use data file and documentation. Accessed on August 31, 2016. [in Korean] www.suneung.re.kr/.

Mincer, Jacob. 1974. Schooling, Experience, and Earnings. Columbia University Press, New York.

Ministry of Education. 2016. "Program for Industrial needs – Matched Education (PRIME): 21 college selected." May 4, 2016. Accessed on August 31, 2016. [in Korean] www.moe.go.kr/web/100026/ko/board/list.do.

OECD. 2012. Closing the Gender Gap. Act Now. OECD Publishing, Paris. December 17, 2012. Access on September 10, 2016. https://dx.doi.org/10.1787/9789264179380-en.

OECD. 2013. Government at a Glance 2013. OECD Publishing, Paris. November 14, 2013. Accessed on September 8, 2016. https://dx.doi.org/10.1787/gov_glance-2013-en.

OECD. 2016. "Labour Force Statistics by Sex and Age (Indicators)." Public-use data file and documentation. Accessed on September 25 2016. http://stats.oecd.org.

Statistics Korea. 2013. Social Indicators in Korea. Statistics of Korea Publishing, Daejeon. March 23, 2016. Accessed on July 19 2016. http://kostat.go.kr/portal/korea/kor_nw/2/6/5/index.board.

The Economist Data Team. 2016. "The Best—and Worst—Places to Be a Working Woman." *The Economist*, May 3, 2016. Access on September 6, 2016.

Tolley, Kim. 2014 The Science Education of American Girls: A Historical Perspective. Routledge, New York.

White House. 2013a. Women and girls in science, technology, engineering, and math (STEM). www.whitehouse.gov/sites/default/files/microsites/ostp/stem_factsheet_2013_07232013.pdf. Accessed October 15, 2015.

White House. 2013b. Educate to Innovate: The 2013 White House science fair. www.whitehouse.gov/issues/education/k-12/educate-innovate. Accessed October 15, 2015.

White House. 2015. Factsheet: President Obama announces over $240 million in new STEM commitments at the 2015 White House Science Fair. www.whitehouse.gov/the-press-office/2015/03/23/fact-sheet-president-obama-announces-over-240-million-new-stem-commitmen. Accessed October 15, 2015.

Wiswall, Matthew, and Basit Zafar. 2015. "Determinants of College Major Choice: Identification Using an Information Experiment." The Review of Economic Studies 82 (2): 791–824.

Woo, Jaeyeon. "Tapping at South Korea's Glass Ceiling." The Wall Street Journal, June 17, 2013. Accessed on September 1, 2016. http://blogs.wsj.com/koreareal-time/2013/06/17/south-korea-struggles-to-welcome-women-at-work/.

World Values Survey. 2016. "World Values Survey (WVS) Wave 6 (2010–2014)." Public-use data file and documentation. Accessed on September 25, 2016. www.world valuessurvey.org.

Zafar, Basit. 2013. "College Major Choice and the Gender Gap." Journal of Human Resources 48 (3): 545–595.

7 Brain drain, circulation, and linkage

Sequence analysis of Korean nationals graduating from Stanford University

Joon Nak Choi and Chuck Eesley

Policy-makers, the media, and the public in Korea have actively discussed the consequences of sending students abroad to study. Studying abroad has long been a salient phenomenon in Korea (see Shin and Choi 2015), and continues to be salient today. Many in Korea have expressed concerns about the "brain drain" generated when students remain overseas after graduation. Such a pattern would exacerbate the demographic crisis that Korea will soon be facing (see Chapter 1 for details), removing highly educated workers from the Korean economy. Furthermore, the brain drain would selectively target individuals with the motivation and talent to study abroad, possibly reducing the creativity and innovativeness of Korean firms and exacerbating their strategic and operational problems in an environment where these characteristics are becoming increasingly critical strategic resources as described in Chapters 1 through 5 of this volume.

Other observers, however, have portrayed a more nuanced view of study abroad. Many Koreans studying abroad return home immediately after graduation, carrying with them the skills they learned overseas. Others return home after working abroad, acquiring further skills and work experience. Either life course generates "brain circulation" that would greatly alleviate the problems that Korean firms are facing today. Koreans who studied and worked abroad would not only return with the human capital they amassed through these experiences, but also an appreciation of the diverse cultures and points of view they experienced abroad. Consequently, they would contribute towards a greater diversity of ideas within Korean firms, and moreover, a greater appreciation for diversity and its potential to generate innovations. Increased diversity and acceptance of differences should increase Korean firms' creativity and responsiveness to uncertainty (see Chapter 1 for a review), increasing their ability to compete in emerging industries and differentiate themselves in established ones as described in Chapters 2 and 3 of this volume. Furthermore, returnees would bring back direct knowledge of foreign markets and their social ties with potential partners and clients found there, greatly facilitating Korean firms' entry into these markets (see Shin and Choi 2015 for a review).

Furthermore, even study abroad outcomes that resemble brain drain at first glance might actually constitute a more benign form of "brain linkage". Shin and Choi (2015, 2016) propose that transmigration generates both human capital (i.e., skills) and social capital (i.e., relationships) that could potentially benefit their countries of origin. Should Korean students choose to remain in the host countries where they studied, they would contribute their human capital towards the host countries' economies, not Korea. Yet, such students would spread information and innovations across Korea and their host countries, and also generate opportunities for cooperation between them. Although the human capital of such students would be lost to the Korean economy, the information flows and opportunities for cooperation they would generate would nevertheless increase the diversity of information circulating within Korea, potentially increasing the creativity and responsiveness to uncertainty of firms and individuals there.

Does study abroad generate brain drain and exacerbate Korea's economic problems? Conversely, does study abroad generate brain circulation and alleviate the same problems? Furthermore, to what extent do cases that look like brain drain at first glance actually constitute brain linkage? To empirically investigate patterns of brain drain, circulation, and linkage in fine-grained detail, this chapter examines Korean citizens who graduated from Stanford University and their work experiences after graduation. This context offers several advantages for the purpose of examining patterns of brain drain, circulation, and linkage. Stanford is well known among prospective students in Korea, and tends to attract some of the most talented Koreans. Also, Stanford offers training across the entire spectrum of academic fields, but nevertheless has a strong focus on the sciences and engineering, and produces graduates in these fields who are heavily recruited by both American and Korean firms. For example, Samsung sponsors Korean student organizations and sports events, largely for the purpose of building relationships with students. Stanford is also located at the epicenter of Silicon Valley's technology ecosystem, and its strong ties with local firms and start-ups facilitate the employment of its graduates there. Consequently, many if not most Korean students at Stanford can choose to either remain in the United States or repatriate. For these reasons, a study of Stanford graduates should provide insights into highly talented Koreans and their careers following graduation, which may range between "brain drain" that would exacerbate the human and social capital shortages described in Chapter 1 to "brain circulation" that would alleviate the same problems.

Study abroad and its consequences for Korea

Study abroad remains an important and highly visible phenomenon within Korean society. As of 2014, 219,543 Korean citizens were studying abroad. While this figure declined from a peak of 262,425 in 2011, it nevertheless remains at roughly 6 percent of Korea's university population.[1] Their preferred destination remains the United States, which hosted 63,710 Korean students in 2014.[2] Universities there are viewed as providing superior quality educations compared with those in Korea, enabling their graduates to advance more rapidly in their careers (Hong and Choi 2012).

Korea has perhaps experienced brain drain more severely than other advanced economies. According to the Brain Drain Index, calculated by the International Institute of Management Development (IMD) so that a score of 0 indicates severe brain drain and 10 indicates no brain drain at all, Korea fluctuated between 3.40 and 5.91 from 2005 to 2013, compared with a range of 6.64 and 7.88 for the United States. What makes brain drain particularly pernicious is that students studying overseas represent some of the brightest young minds in Korea. According to the Korea Trade-Investment Promotion Agency (KOTRA),

> the leakage of high-quality labor weakens our research and development capabilities, which translates to weakened competitiveness for Korean firms and the nation as a whole, and may create an extreme scenario where we must rely on foreign labor and technology.[3]

However, there is also evidence that study abroad has generated brain circulation among Koreans. By repatriating graduates after upgrading their skills, brain circulation can greatly enhance the quality of human capital available to Korean businesses (Kirkegaard 2007; see also Saxenian 2006). Koreans who studied in the United States highlight this pattern. Although such students might be expected to remain in the United States, which is an advanced economy that has historically been welcoming of skilled immigrants, several studies have found that they nevertheless tend to return home more than they remain abroad. Analyzing US government data, Kirkegaard (2007) found that a large proportion of Korean students in the United States return home, with a smaller proportion choosing to remain in the United States. Surveying Korean students in the United States, Hong and Cho (2012) found that 56.7 percent intended to return to Korea for their first jobs and that an additional 12.7 percent intended to return at a later time. Also surveying Korean students in the United States, Shin and Choi (2015) found that students viewed a return to Korea moderately favorably, averaging a response of 3.31 on a 5-point Likert scale. Brain circulation not only provides human capital benefits, but also social capital benefits as well. Shin and Choi (2015, 2016) propose that Koreans who studied abroad can maintain the relationships they had built in their host countries when they return home. Such "transnational bridges" facilitate communication and cooperation across social and geographic boundaries dividing countries from one another (Storper and Venables 2004) and help firms operating overseas adapt to foreign cultures and practices (Zaheer 1995). Such individuals can also broker information and resource exchanges, spread innovations and facilitate other forms of cooperation (Bathelt et al. 2004; Saxenian 2006; Whittington et al. 2009).

Although policy-makers, the media, and academics are starting to recognize brain drain, circulation, and even linkage as important phenomena, key questions regarding these patterns remain unanswered. To be sure, much attention has already been paid to these patterns. Studies conducted in the United States (e.g., Kirkegaard 2007) have largely viewed Korean students as human capital, and have investigated ways of retaining them after graduation by improving the optional practical training (OPT) program. Studies conducted in Korea have also viewed these students as human capital, and sought to measure and eventually alleviate brain drain. For instance, the Science and Technology Policy Institute, a government-supported think tank, calculated a measure of brain drain (i.e., an output/input index) focusing on students in science and engineering. The same study also surveyed Korean citizens studying science and engineering in the United States, and investigated their motivations and chances of remaining there or returning home (Hong and Cho 2012). Shin and Choi (2015) also surveyed and interviewed Korean students in the United States, not only to determine their motivations for remaining there or repatriating, but also to assess their potential to bridge Korea with the United States. While these studies have provided deep insights regarding current students' motivations and intentions, they have yet to investigate how their careers develop and where they end up. Reviewing Shin and Choi (2015), Park (2016, p.1-2) highlights gaps in the current literature:

> The book stops short of fully explaining what will make "brain circulation" a reality, largely because it focuses on the potential of the labor pools. Thus, the question still remains: Under what conditions does the transnational embeddedness examined here—social ties, transnational aspirations, and familiarity with cultures—lead to actual instances of transnational bridging? Since we cannot assume that transnational bridging is automatically established ... this question begs further empirical analysis.

Still missing is an in-depth study of empirical patterns of brain drain, circulation, and especially linkage.

Instead of taking a deductive hypothesis testing approach aimed at theory confirmation, this chapter will take an inductive approach aimed at theory construction. While anecdotes about Korean graduates of American universities and their work histories abound, few if any studies have systematically examined their life courses after graduating. To conduct such a systematic examination, work histories are examined using sequence analysis, a technique for identifying empirical regularities in life course trajectories by grouping individuals with similar work or life histories (e.g., Abbott and Tsay 2000). The objective is to reduce the complexity inherent in work histories to identify, describe, and eventually theorize the most salient elements. The remainder of this chapter will use this technique to examine the work histories of 89 Korean graduates of Stanford University and find salient empirical patterns, and will conclude with the theoretical implications of these findings.

Empirical analysis

Data and sample

This chapter uses data from the Stanford Innovation Survey (Eesley 2011). Alumni surveys have become increasingly popular in academic research. Institutions whose alumni were recently surveyed include Stanford University (Dobrev and Barnett 2005), Harvard Business School (Lerner and Malmendier 2009), Iowa State University (Jolly et al. 2009), University of Virginia (Lenox et al. 2014), Tsinghua University (Eesley, Li and Yang 2016), and the Massachusetts Institute of Technology (Eesley and Roberts 2012; Eesley, Hsu, and Roberts 2014; Roberts and Eesley 2009). The Stanford Innovation Survey (along with those at UVA and Tsinghua University) was based in part on the MIT alumni survey (Hsu et al. 2007). The Stanford Innovation Survey went out to 143,482 out of 191,332 total living Stanford alumni in 2011. The 47,850 uncontacted alumni either left no contact information with Stanford University or were on a "do not contact" list typically including of some of the most successful alumni. Of the 143,482 contacted alumni, 27,783 (19.4 percent) responded and were included in the data. Some categories of alumni were more likely to respond than others: women were 5.1 percent more likely to respond than men, and graduates of the Education and Medical schools were more likely to respond while those from the Law and Engineering schools were less likely. Furthermore, each year elapsed since graduation increased response rates by 0.9 percent, indicating that recent graduates were much less likely to respond (see Eesley and Miller 2012). Overall, the survey was conducted over a well-defined population of comparable individuals in multiple industries, and it was administered through official university channels and hence more trustworthy to the respondents.

This chapter focuses on the 89 respondents of the Stanford Innovation Survey who were Republic of Korea citizens as Stanford students.[4] Thirteen respondents received Bachelor's degrees, 61 received at least one Master's or professional degree, and 41 received PhDs or postdoctoral training from Stanford; 28 received multiple types of degrees. These figures are consistent with Stanford accepting far more international applicants for graduate than undergraduate study. As of October 2011, foreign students (i.e., without United States citizenship or permanent residency) constituted 32.7 percent of Stanford graduate students, but only 7.6 percent of undergraduates. These figures increased from those of October 1998, when foreigners constituted 28.2 percent of graduate students and 4.6 percent of undergraduates.[5] The scarcity of Korean respondents might indicate that they were systematically less likely to respond than American or other foreign respondents; if roughly 2,000 Korean citizens graduated from Stanford, and if 1,500 could be contacted, the response rate would only be 6 percent compared with the 19.4 percent for the broader alumni base.[6] A plausible explanation is that Korean citizens tended to have graduated more recently and were less likely to respond. The number of Korean citizens studying in the United States skyrocketed from 1999 through 2008, before dropping somewhat through 2011 (Shin and Choi 2015). Indeed, the number of Korean graduate students at Stanford doubled from 1997–1998 (181) to 2007–2008 (363), suggesting that many of Stanford's Korean alumni are recent graduates. Respondent graduation dates as reported in the survey are consistent with this notion, as the average estimated undergraduate graduation year for all survey respondents was 1985, while the average for Korean respondents was 1999. Considering that a one-year increment was associated with a 0.9 percent decline in the response rate (see Eesley and Miller 2012), the 14-year difference on average between 1985 and 1999 should lower response rates by 12.6 percent. This is almost exactly the observed difference in response rate between Korean alumni and the alumni base as a whole. Further evidence indicating that Koreans were not systematically adverse to responding to the survey was that Korean respondents indicated greater willingness to answer follow-up surveys than respondents as a whole (56.2 percent versus 48.4 percent).

Data coding

For each of the 89 Korean respondents to the survey, we coded their educational experiences and work histories by country and type, creating 477 discrete spells. Respondents provided the order, most starting dates, and some ending dates for these spells, so that spells could be sequenced into discrete work histories.

Countries of spells

The most common countries for specific spells were the United States (198 spells) and Korea (169 spells). While only seven additional spells were explicitly associated with other countries, 84 were associated with non-Korean multinational corporations (MNCs) operating across the world. The locations for these spells could not be determined, even though they most likely occurred in the United States. Thus, they were coded separately and associated with MNCs.

Types of spells

Respondents provided roughly equal numbers of educational (243) and work experiences (234). Educational experiences at Stanford were not distinguished from those received elsewhere. The majority of respondents received training in engineering or computer science, as 56 (62.9 percent of 89 respondents) received a BA/BS or equivalent, 56 (62.9 percent) received a MA/MS or equivalent, and 36 (40.4 percent) received a PhD or equivalent. Smaller numbers received training in biology and medicine, the humanities or social science (including economics) and business (Table 7.1).

Regarding work experiences, the most numerous (53) involved a research or teaching position at a university or research institute. Nearly as many (49) took place at MNCs in the technology sector. The third largest category (28) involved working at a Korean *chaebol* (Table 7.2).

The Stanford Innovation Survey also provided information about respondent participation in start-ups either as investors or board members. As these experiences differed from actual work experiences, we did not include them in the sequence analyses, but examine them separately.

Overall, the majority of Korean survey respondents pursued careers in engineering and computer science, and in academia in some cases. This is

Table 7.1 Educational spells

Educational spells	Count
Associate's Degree in Science	1
Bachelor's Degree in Biomed	8
Bachelor's Degree in Business	2
Bachelor's Degree in Engineering and Computer Science	56
Bachelor's Degree in Humanities	5
Bachelor's Degree in Law	1
Bachelor's Degree in Operations Research And Statistics	2
Bachelor's Degree in Science	7
Bachelor's Degree in Social Sciences	6
Juris Doctor	3
Master's Degree in Biomedical	3
Master's Degree in Business	3
Master's Degree in Education	6
Master's Degree in Engineering And Computer Science	56
Master's Degree in Humanities	6
Master's Degree in Law	2
Master's Degree in Operations Research And Statistics	4
Master's Degree in Science	4
Master's Degree in Social Sciences	2
Master's of Business Administration	6
Medical Doctor	3
Nondegree Training in Engineering or Computer Science	1
Nondegree Training in the Humanities	1
PhD in Biomedical	4
PhD in Education	3
PhD in Engineering and Computer Science	36
PhD in Humanities	3
PhD in Law	1
PhD in Operations Research and Statistics	3
PhD in Science	4
Postdoctoral Fellowship in Biomedical	1
Total	243

consistent with Stanford's focus on engineering and computer science, as well as the previously documented tendency of Koreans studying in the United States to enter academia (see Hong and Choi 2012).

Methodology

We use a simplified version of sequence analysis that groups individuals by the country and major of undergraduate spells, rather than using a quantitative clustering algorithm. Sequence analysis typically consists of two steps: code the life experiences of relevant individuals into appropriate dummy variables, and use a clustering algorithm to group individuals with similar experiences (Abbott and Tsay 2000). We initially used this approach, using hierarchical clustering following Powell and Sandholtz (2012). This analysis, however, generated clusters

Table 7.2 Work spells

Work spells	Count
Job in Biotech	9
Job in *Chaebol*	28
Job in Consulting	16
Job in Corporate	6
Job in Education	3
Job in Finance	7
Job in Government	4
Job in Law	1
Job in the Nonprofit Sector	3
Job in Other	1
Job in Technology	49
Job in a University	53
Job in Venture Capital	8
Start-up (founder or employee)	32
Start-up (investor or advisor)	14
Total	234

of individuals that could as easily be identified by simply grouping individuals by their undergraduate majors and sometimes country. Thus, we examined six different clusters of respondents. Five of these clusters corresponded with under-graduate majors: engineering or computer science in Korea ($n=47$), engineering or computer science in the United States ($n=10$), biology or medicine ($n=9$), the humanities ($n=6$) and the social sciences (mainly economics) and business ($n=8$). Another cluster corresponded to academic careers primarily in the natural sciences ($n=8$). Respondents who did not fit into any of these categories ($n=3$) were excluded from the analysis.

Sequence analyses of respondent clusters

Engineering and computer science undergraduates in Korea

This cluster includes 46 respondents who conducted their undergraduate studies in engineering and computer science in Korea, and one additional respondent who did not list an undergraduate degree but obtained a Master's degree in engineering in Korea. Figure 7.1 summarizes their career progressions over time. In this diagram, boxes represent spells and arrows represent transitions between spells; the size of the arrow indicates the frequency of the transition. The sequence of career transitions is laid out from left to right, with the leftmost spell (i.e., an undergraduate degree in engineering or computer science in Korea) being the starting point and the rightmost spells being career endpoints. As many respondents were still early in their careers, late career transitions were observed less often than early career transitions. To reduce the complexity of this diagram, transitions that occurred only once are not shown.

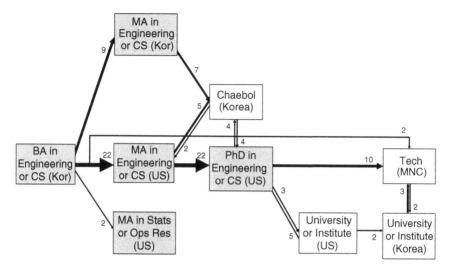

Figure 7.1 Respondents who started with a BA in Engineering in Korea.

As might be expected, students generally progressed from an undergraduate degree in Korea to a Master's degree in the United States, typically at Stanford, before receiving PhDs in the United States. Another common sequence was for students to receive a Master's degree in Korea before working at one of the *chaebol*, and then progressing onwards to Master's or PhDs in the United States, typically at Stanford. What is interesting is that many respondents returned to Korea to work for the *chaebol* after graduating from Master's degrees or PhDs in the United States, suggesting that *chaebol*-based economic opportunities may have driven brain circulation. Indeed, the *chaebol* may even have sponsored these individuals' graduate degrees on the condition that they return afterwards, a possibility not captured in our data. Nevertheless, the most common transition for PhDs was to work for a MNC in the technology field, which many would interpret as brain drain. PhDs also transitioned into academic positions in the United States. Interestingly, two of these individuals ended up at academic positions in Korea, a pattern that is also seen among other academics outside of the biomedical field.

Engineering and computer science undergraduates in the United States

This cluster includes 10 respondents who conducted their undergraduate studies in engineering and computer science in the United States. Figure 7.2 summarizes their career progressions over time. In this diagram, boxes represent spells and arrows represent transitions between spells; the size of the arrow indicates the frequency of the transition.

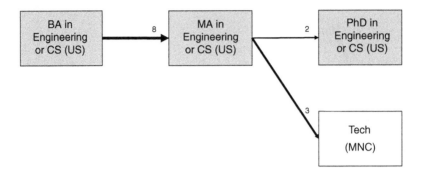

Figure 7.2 Respondents who started with a BA in Engineering in the United States.

Contrary to otherwise similar respondents who had earned their under-graduate degrees in Korea, these respondents did not return to Korea, ending up in PhD programs in the United States or at technology MNCs. Note that none of these respondents had held United States citizenship at the time, although they may have held permanent residency.

Biology and medical students

This cluster includes nine respondents who conducted their undergraduate studies in biology in the United States or Korea. Figure 7.3 shows their career trajectories.

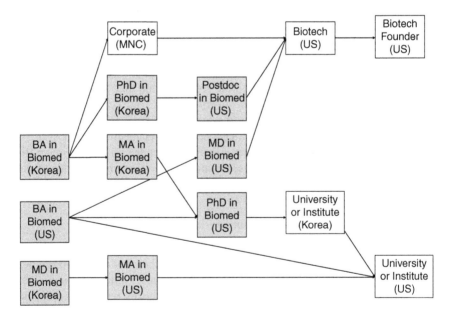

Figure 7.3 Respondents who started with a BA in Biology or Medicine.

These respondents progressed along career trajectories that appeared to vary substantially at first glance. No two respondents made the same transition, noting that the sample itself was miniscule. Consequently, transitions that occurred only once are shown in Figure 7.3. Despite their apparent uniqueness, these trajectories may share two important underlying similarities. First, respondents end up working either in the biotechnology industry or an academic institution. Second, respondents move from Korea to the United States, at times accepting a decline in pay and status (i.e., from an MD in Korea to an MA in the United States). In contrast, respondents typically do not return to Korea. To the extent that inferences can be drawn from a miniscule sample of only nine respondents, it would appear that brain drain may predominate over brain circulation in this field.

Academic careers in the natural and social sciences

This cluster includes seven respondents who conducted their undergraduate studies in the natural or social sciences either in the United States or Korea. Figure 7.4 shows their career trajectories.

These respondents progressed along a very consistent career track. Having earned Bachelor's and Master's degrees in Korea, they often received a PhD from a university in the United States, typically at Stanford. Some respondents transitioned immediately into an academic position in Korea, while others transitioned first into an academic position in the United States before returning to Korea. What is interesting is that all seven respondents ended up in academic positions in Korea, mirroring the same pattern seen among engineering and computer science students who received their undergraduate degrees in Korea. While inferences can only be drawn from such a small sample to a limited extent, the consistency found within this category may nevertheless suggest that brain circulation is widespread among academics outside of biology and medicine. Indeed, many if not most Korean universities continue to preferentially hire returnees with PhDs from top American universities such as Stanford, although the pattern might be changing to some degree.

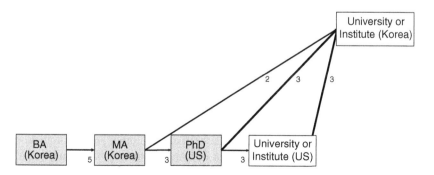

Figure 7.4 Respondents in Academia not in Engineering, Biomed, and the Humanities.

Non-academic careers in the social sciences

This cluster includes five respondents who majored in economics, two respondents who majored in business, and one who majored in operations research. These respondents followed career trajectories that varied in the specifics but followed the same general pattern. Of these eight respondents, six worked in finance or consulting at some point and two worked in venture capital. These respondents were also quite entrepreneurial, with five having started companies of their own.

Half of these respondents received their undergraduate degrees in Korea, and the other half in the United States. Like computer science and engineering graduates, three of four respondents who started in Korea tended to remain engaged and active there, indeed founding start-ups based there. In contrast, only one of four respondents who started in the United States returned to Korea in any role, although the one respondent who did perhaps played an important role in promoting entrepreneurship in Korea by joining a venture capital firm and founding a consulting firm there.

Humanities undergraduates and graduate students

The final cluster includes six respondents who studied subjects in the humanities as undergraduate, Master's, or PhD students. Their career trajectories are varied and difficult to generalize from, perhaps highlighting the difficulty of pursuing careers in their field of study. Nevertheless, three of the six respondents ended up in academic jobs, two in the United States and one in Korea. Two others ended up leaving the humanities despite earning graduate degrees in this field, and ended up in business careers.

Theoretical implications

To the extent that inferences can be drawn from such a small sample, our findings offer two broad insights. First, there may be substantial differences in career trajectories across these fields, particularly in respondents remaining in the United States or repatriating to Korea, depending on economic opportunity. On one hand, Korea may have offered respondents particularly in engineering and the natural sciences ample opportunities to return. Anecdotal evidence suggests that the *chaebol* aggressively and effectively recruited Korean students abroad, while Korean universities showed a preference for hiring US PhDs. In the latter case, the difficulty of earning tenure at US universities may have contributed towards the decision of many respondents to return home. On the other hand, Korea may have offered few real opportunities to respondents in biology and the natural sciences, considering what appeared to be their steady flow out of Korea. These patterns perhaps suggest that the question of brain drain versus circulation must be examined within specific fields or economic contexts, as the question of repatriation is strongly affected by opportunity structures at home and abroad. Patterns found within one field may not necessarily apply towards another field.

Second, students who earned undergraduate degrees in Korea may have been more likely to return than otherwise similar students who earned undergraduate degrees in the United States. This pattern remained consistent across fields as different as engineering and business. These findings hint that the pattern Shin and Choi (2015) found among *chogi yuhak* students—who left Korea to study abroad during secondary school—may also apply more broadly towards all undergraduates. One *chogi yuhak* student interviewed by Shin and Choi (2015, p. 81) noted that she had grown distant from Korean culture during her undergraduate study overseas:

> I saw that my friends learned different things [than I did] as they passed through college in Korea. They drank a lot and treated seniors and juniors differently than they do in the U.S.... People change a great deal during college life. My friends are like that. Someone who attended college in the U.S. will need much time to adjust to this culture. I am worried about this. (translated from Korean)

These findings hint at the importance of the intense socialization that occurs during college in Korea, and for males, during military service. Individuals who experienced such socialization before leaving Korea may be more likely to return home than those who have not.

Examining brain linkage via start-up investments and board memberships

Although sequence analysis provides insights regarding brain drain versus brain circulation, it does not provide compelling evidence of brain linkage. This analysis cannot identify respondent interactions with Korea short of a move back to Korea. Thus, someone who remains in the United States and has no professional contact with Korea would look identical to someone based in the United States but actively engaged with professional contacts back home.

The Stanford Innovation Survey provides additional data, however, that may identify such brain linkages. Beyond asking respondents about start-ups they have founded or joined, the survey also asks about the start-ups they have funded or advised as board members. Investors and board members do not necessarily have to be geographically collocated with their affiliated start-ups. Thus, someone based in the United States could potentially fund or advise a start-up in Korea, paralleling the transnational relationships Saxenian (2006) highlighted between Silicon Valley and emerging technology clusters in Taiwan, Israel, and India. Such relationships are economically important, not only seeding emerging technology clusters with capital and know-how but also spreading best practices and an innovation-oriented culture. Should such cases be found in the survey, they would constitute evidence of brain linkage.

Among the 89 Korean respondents to the survey, six of them (6.7 percent) have funded and/or served as board members of Korea-based technology start-ups. Four of these cases correspond to the 46 respondents who finished their undergraduate studies in engineering and computer science in Korea (8.7 percent). All four of these cases constitute brain circulation rather than linkage, however, as they returned to Korea and took jobs either in *chaebol* or academic institutions before funding or advising start-ups. One case corresponding to the 10 respondents who received undergraduate degrees in engineering and computer science in the United States, however, appears to constitute brain linkage. This respondent worked for a technology-oriented MNC while funding a Korea-based start-up. Later, this respondent moved to Korea and founded a technology start-up there. Another case corresponding to business and business-oriented social science majors joined a US-based management consulting firm before investing in a Korea-based start-up. This person eventually became a venture capitalist in the United States before founding a start-up in Korea. These two cases appear to represent brain linkage, where a person in the United States contributed funding and expertise to Korea-based start-ups, playing a transnational bridging role.

To the extent that inferences can be drawn from only two cases, brain linkage may be economically significant. As Saxenian (2006) argues, a relatively small number of immigrants versed in Silicon Valley's innovation culture can seed their home countries with the capital, know-how, and entrepreneurial attitude needed to establish technology clusters there. The two respondents representing brain linkages played this role, moving from remotely funding and advising start-ups in Korea to actually founding start-ups there. This finding also suggests that brain linkage may be a precursor to brain circulation, assuming that economic opportunities exist in Korea. Although brain linkage was only demonstrated for two respondents out of 89, many of the other respondents could not have functioned in that role as they had already returned home (i.e., brain circulation). Also, many respondents were not in technology-related fields and could not have funded or advised start-ups. Such individuals, however, very well may have functioned in the brain linkage role in a different way that was not captured by the survey, which focused on innovation and entrepreneurship.

Conclusion

An examination of the careers of 89 Korean respondents to the Stanford Innovation Survey finds evidence of brain drain, circulation, and linkage. Prior studies (e.g., Hong and Cho 2012; Shin and Choi 2015, 2016) suggested that many, if not the majority of, Korean students in the United States were interested in returning to Korea if the economic opportunity was there. Empirical analysis of survey respondents indicates that economic opportunities indeed encourage brain circulation, as respondents in fields where Korean employers offered relatively attractive opportunities (e.g., engineering and academia) tended to return home at higher rates than respondents in fields where appropriate opportunities were lacking in Korea (e.g., biology and medicine). The findings also suggest that Koreans who received their undergraduate degrees in Korea are more likely to return than those who received undergraduate degrees in the United States, reflecting the greater time spent in Korea and the greater amount of socialization into Korean culture experienced over this period. Overall, brain drain is more likely for respondents lacking economic opportunities and socialization in the Korean context.

Just because a respondent chose to stay in the United States, however, did not necessarily mean that the respondent constituted brain drain. At least two respondents who remained in the United States actively contributed their capital and expertise towards start-ups in Korea, before eventually moving there to found start-ups of their own. While two cases might appear to be a small proportion of the overall sample, many other respondents had either returned home as instances of brain circulation, or worked in fields where they were unlikely to be involved with start-ups. Indeed, it is important to remember that many if not most Koreans who remained in the United States after graduation might have performed similar bridging roles in their own fields, in ways that were not captured by the Stanford Innovation Survey. Overall, these findings suggest that even cases of apparent brain drain might actually represent economically beneficial cases of brain circulation.

These findings are subject to several limitations. Stanford University students are not representative of the broader population of Korean students studying in the USA in two ways. Attending one of the most recognizable and highest-status universities, these students may differ *ex ante* from the broader population. Furthermore, they may face different opportunity sets ex post than the population. Consequently, our findings should be interpreted within this context. Data completeness is another concern, as the survey asked respondents only about their first jobs, most recent jobs and the most important job in between. Individuals with a longer career history may have had other relevant job spells that were not captured by the survey. Perhaps most importantly, our findings are based on a miniscule sample of 89 individuals, and proper caution must be exercised when extrapolating our findings to a broader population.

There are several other factors relevant to brain drain, circulation, and linkage that were not examined in this chapter. Although we identify individuals who were Korean citizens as of the time when they attended Stanford University, we cannot determine if they held permanent residency in the USA. Having the legal right to abode would have certainly affected their post-graduation decisions, although many non-resident graduates in engineering and the sciences would have been eligible to stay in the USA under the Optional Practical Training Program. Gender would have also affected their future plans, with women potentially being less willing to return to a Korea that has remained more of a patriarchy than the USA. Similarly, individuals with family in the USA would have had an incentive to remain there, while others with family in Korea would have an incentive to return. The role of these factors represents fertile grounds for future research.

Notes

1 ICEF Monitor. 2015. "Number of Korean Students Abroad Declines for Third Straight Year." http://monitor.icef.com/2015/02/number-korean-students-abroad-declines-third-straight-year/.
2 Institute for International Education, 2015. "International Students in the United States." www.iie.org/Services/Project-Atlas/United-States/International-Students-In-US. See also Rubin (2014).
3 Kim Youngjin, as cited in an ETNews.com article by Guen Il Yoon (www.etnews.com/20150102000040).
4 One additional respondent who held both Korean and American citizenship was dropped from the analysis.
5 Bechtel International Center, Stanford University. 2016. "Stanford International Student Statistics." http://icenter.stanford.edu/about_us/student_stats/.
6 Although the number of Korean citizens who received Stanford degrees was not available, a rough estimate was found by adding the number of enrolled Korean graduate students reported by the Bechtel International Center in 2011, 2007, 2002, and 1997 (1,126) to the relatively few undergraduates. This figure was known to be 68 as of 2011. While undergraduate figures for past years were not reported, the 2007–2011 period represented a peak for Korean students (see Shin and Choi 2015) and 250 for the 1997–2011 period might be a conservative estimate. Thus, 2000 might be a reasonable estimate of the number of Korean graduates from Stanford, indicating a response rate of 4.5 percent.

References

Abbott, Andrew and Angela Tsay. 2000. "Sequence Analysis and Optimal Matching Methods in Sociology: Review and Prospect." Sociological Methods and Research 29: 3–33.
Bathelt, Harald, Anders Malmberg, and Peter Maskell. 2004. "Clusters and knowledge: local buzz, global pipelines and the process of knowledge creation." Progress in Human Geography 28(1): 31–56.
Dobrev, S.D. and W.P. Barnett. 2005. "Organizational roles and transition to entrepreneurship." Academy of Management Journal 48(3): 433–449.
Eesley, C.; J.B. Li, and D. Yang. 2016. Does Institutional Change in Universities Influence High-Tech Entrepreneurship?: Evidence from China's Project 985. Organization Science 27(2) (March-April): 446–461.
Eesley, C.E., Hsu, D.H. and Roberts, E.B., 2014. The contingent effects of top management teams on venture performance: Aligning founding team composition with innovation strategy and commercialization environment. Strategic Management Journal 35(12): 1798–1817.
Eesley, C.E. and Roberts, E.B., 2012. Are You Experienced or Are You Talented?: When Does Innate Talent Versus Experience Explain Entrepreneurial Performance?. Strategic Entrepreneurship Journal 6(3): 207–219.
Eesley, Charles and William F. Miller. 2012. "Impact: Stanford University's Economic Impact via Innovation and Entrepreneurship." Survey report.
Eesley, Chuck. 2011. "Stanford Innovation Survey: Creation of Non-profit Organizations." Referenced at https://ecorner.stanford.edu/article/stanford-innovation-survey-creation-of-non-profit-organizations/.
Hong, Sungmin, and Gawon Cho. 2012. "Entry and Exit Patterns of Sciences and Engineering Human Resources in 2012." Science and Technology Policy Institute (Korea).

Hsu, D.H., Roberts, E.B. and Eesley, C.E., 2007. Entrepreneurs from technology-based universities: Evidence from MIT. Research Policy 36(5): 768–788.

Jolly, Robert W., Li Yu and Peter Orazem. 2009. "After They Graduate: An Overview of the Iowa State University Alumni Survey." Iowa State University Economics Working Paper Series. Working Paper # 09002.

Kierkegaard, Jacob F. 2007. The accelerating decline in America's high-skill workforce. Policy Analyses in International Economics No. 84. Washington: Peterson Institute.

Lenox, M., King, A., Eesley, C., Mehedi, A. 2014. The Economic Impact of Entrepreneurial Alumni: A Case Study of the University of Virginia. Available at: http://web3.darden.virginia.edu/uva-alumni.

Lerner, Josh and Ulrike Malmendier. 2009. "With a Little Help from My (Random) Friends: Success and Failure in Post-Business School Entrepreneurship." Harvard Business School Working Paper.

Park, Keumjae. 2016. Book Review of Global Talent: Skilled Labor as Social Capital in Korea. International Migration Review.

Powell, Walter, and Kurt W. Sandholtz. 2012. "Amphibious entrepreneurs and the emergence of organizational forms." Strategic Entrepreneurship Journal 6(2): 94–115.

Roberts, E.B. and Charles Eesley. 2009. "Entrepreneurial Impact: The Role of MIT." Ewing Marion Kauffman Foundation.

Rubin, Kyna. 2014. "The Changing Tide of South Korean Student Flows." International Educator (March/April), 28–34.

Saxenian, AnnaLee. 2006. The New Argonauts: Regional Advantage in a Global Economy. Cambridge, MA: Harvard University Press.

Shin, Gi-Wook and Joon Nak Choi. 2015. Global Talent: Towards a New Model of Engaging Skilled Foreigners in Korea. Stanford University Press.

Shin, Gi-Wook and Joon Nak Choi. 2016. "From Brain Drain to Brain Linkage: Korean Students Abroad as Transnational Bridges." In Internationalizing Higher Education in Korea: Challenges and Opportunities in Comparative Perspective. Ed. Yeon Cheon Oh, Gi-Wook Shin and Rennie Moon. Washington, DC: The Brookings Institution Press.

Storper, Michael and Anthony J. Venables. 2004. "Buzz: Face-to-Face Contact and the Urban Economy." Journal of Economic Geography 4: 351–370.

Whittington, Kjersten Bunker, Jason Owen-Smith and Walter W. Powell. 2009. "Networks, Propinquity, and Innovation in Knowledge-Intensive Industries." Administrative Science Quarterly 54(1): 90–122.

Zaheer, Srilata. 1995. "Overcoming the Liability of Foreignness." Academy of Management Journal 48(2): 341–363.

8 A comparative analysis of Asian versus Asian American entrepreneurship

Evidence from Stanford University alumni

Yong Suk Lee and Chuck Eesley

One of the most notable features of entrepreneurship and innovation in Silicon Valley is the role Asian immigrants have played in technology entrepreneurship and innovation (Saxenian 1999). However, across the Pacific Ocean, many Asian countries are lamenting the lack of entrepreneurship in their homelands and have been actively trying to spur entrepreneurship and innovation through various government initiatives. Returnees from studying abroad in North America and Europe (see Chapter 7) can support such efforts by bringing back innovative technologies and business practices from their Silicon Valley origins (see Saxenian 2006). Given this context, differences between less-assimilated Asians and more-assimilated Asian Americans become salient, as the former are more likely to return to Asia (see Chapter 7 of this volume; Shin and Choi 2015).

This chapter examines whether the entrepreneurship rates of Asians and Asian Americans are significantly different, and if so, why. As the two population groups are likely to be very different, simply comparing the entrepreneurship rates of Asians and Asian Americans is unlikely to explain the discrepancy in entrepreneurship between the two groups. This chapter's objective is to shed light on this question by examining the entrepreneurship patterns using a relatively homogenous sample—Stanford University alumni. We use a unique survey to examine entrepreneurial activities by Stanford University graduates, who have traditionally played an important role in Silicon Valley entrepreneurship. In doing so, we aim to explore some of the underlying reasons behind the differential patterns of entrepreneurship between these Asians and Asian Americans.

A critical constraint in studying entrepreneurship, especially the determinants of entrepreneurship, is that we generally only observe entrepreneurs after they become entrepreneurs. For instance, data on start-ups often exist only for the sub-set of firms that succeed and go public. Survey data on entrepreneurs often suffer from small sample problems or similar selection issues as entrepreneurs are only identified ex post. Moreover, empirical analysis surrounding the determinants of immigrant entrepreneurship has been difficult because of the scarcity of relevant data. One of the main contributions of this chapter is the examination of a representative sample of all Stanford University graduates since the 1930s, *regardless* of whether they became entrepreneurs or not. Moreover, the detailed demographic information in the survey allows us to explore both across and within ethnicity differences in entrepreneurship.

Using the Stanford alumni data, we examine whether Asians on average are more or less likely to become an entrepreneur, invest as an angel investor or venture capital, or become an entrepreneur turned investor. We separately examine Asian Americans from non-American Asians to gauge the importance of culture and immigration for entrepreneurial activity. (In the rest of this chapter, we will simply refer to non-American Asians as Asians). When the data allow, we investigate Asian sub-groups, in particular, Stanford University graduates from Korea, Japan, China, India, and the rest of Asia. The literature has found individual optimism and parental entrepreneurship to be an important determinant of entrepreneurship. We examine how different such characteristics are among the different ethnic and nationality groups and whether those characteristics can explain the difference in entrepreneurial outcome. Another question we explore is whether education at universities influences entrepreneurial choices beyond individual and family factors. Pre-existing differences in entrepreneurial activity within the Asian ethnic sub-groups could change as foreign Asian students obtain US university education and take advantage of the university's entrepreneurship programs. Stanford University introduced major entrepreneurship programs in the mid-1990s at the business school and the engineering school. Both programs offered entrepreneurship courses and experiential learning to students. We examine whether participation in those programs reduces any pre-existing gaps in entrepreneurship based on ethnicity and nationality. In short, this chapter aims to shed light on the importance of individual, family, and educational factors in determining entrepreneurial choice among Asians in a university setting.

Related literature on ethnicity and entrepreneurship

The literature has widely documented the difference in the rate and patterns of entrepreneurship by ethnicity or immigrant status in the USA. Fairlie (1999) finds that family background explains the significantly lower rates of black entrepreneurship in the USA. Fairlie and Robb (2007) further find that the lower performance of black entrepreneurship is a result of lack of training in family businesses. Immigrants, especially Asian immigrants are often hailed as more entrepreneurial. Indeed the statistics indicate high levels of Korean or Indian entrepreneurship in the USA. However, such immigrant entrepreneurship is often clustered into certain industries, for example, the dry cleaning industry for Koreans and motels for Indians, which are unlikely to result in high-growth entrepreneurship (Kerr and Mandorff 2015). Nonetheless, studies on Silicon Valley entrepreneurship highlight the roles immigrants have played in founding high-growth technology ventures (Saxenian 1999, 2006). Aldrich and Zimmer (1986) argue that entrepreneurs are driven by connections to opportunities, and highlight the importance of social networks as the source of entrepreneurial opportunities. Ethnicity is among the most important social networks for entrepreneurial opportunities, and the clusters of ethnic entrepreneurship in the USA represent the reciprocal relationship between ethnicity and entrepreneurship (Aldrich and Waldinger 1990). Our study examines a particular form of ethnic entrepreneurship by focusing on Stanford University alumni, and examines how entrepreneurship varies depending on immigrant status, despite being of the same ethnicity. Our finding that Asian Americans have higher rates of entrepreneurship, but that the rate of entrepreneurship for Asians is substantially lower, indicates that the relationship between ethnicity and entrepreneurship can flexibly change depending on immigration status.

The entrepreneurship literature has examined various factors that affect entrepreneurship, from funding sources (Kerr et al. 2010; Samila and Sorenson 2011), housing collateral (Adelino et al. 2015), family (Bertrand and Schoar 2006), to peers (Lerner and Malmendier 2013). More closely related to this chapter is the literature that examines the importance of culture as a determinant for economic outcome. However, quantifying culture is challenging and the literature has often used immigrant history, for example, parent's original country, to proxy for culture (Fernandez 2010; Guiso et al. 2004; Alesina and Giuliano 2013). The findings of our chapter show that such an approach should be viewed with caution as entrepreneurial activities of individuals of the same ethnicity, age, and very similar educational background differ significantly in their career choices depending on US citizenship status.

The Stanford University Innovation Survey

The Stanford University Innovation Survey (see Chapter 7 for details on the survey) was conducted to better understand the economic impacts Stanford alumni have played in terms of entrepreneurship and innovation. The survey is particularly useful for analyzing entrepreneurial patterns across ethnicity as it covers all students regardless of entrepreneurship status. Often entrepreneurship data are only available for eventual entrepreneurs and publicly listed companies, and information on those who do not become entrepreneurs or do not go public is hard to find. The sample of Stanford alumni is unlikely to be representative of the general population. However, understanding entrepreneurship activity among higher education students is critical to understanding the role of potentially high-growth entrepreneurship. Scholars have emphasized the importance of differentiating high-growth versus low-growth start-ups. Stanford University's role in technology entrepreneurship and many high-growth start-ups provides a unique opportunity to examine high-growth potential start-ups. Other studies have used other alumni surveys from top-tier universities (MIT, Stanford, Harvard, and Chicago) in examining how the broader social environment influences entrepreneurship. Out of the respondents, nearly 8,000 reported being entrepreneurs who founded any type of organization (for-profit or non-profit) and 4,290 said they had founded an incorporated business.

An innovation ecosystem requires not only creative entrepreneurs but also active investors. Moreover, one of Silicon Valley's unique features is the abundance of entrepreneurs who become angel investors or form or join a venture capital. These "entrepreneur investors" may better identify potentially successful start-ups and guide start-ups towards success at various stages of growth. The Stanford survey not only asks one's entrepreneurship status, but also whether one invested in start-ups as an angel investor or venture capitalist. We are thus able to examine whether one was an angel or VC investor, or an entrepreneur investor, in addition to one's entrepreneurship status, that is, whether one found a new organization. Responses include data on 2,798 individuals who were early employees (16 percent of the alumni), 349 venture capital investors, and 2,572 angel investors. Some 3,600 respondents, 18 percent, said they had been on a private company board of directors.

A particularly important aspect of the Stanford Innovation Survey is the rich information on ethnicity and nationality of the students with a particular emphasis on Asians, which this chapter probes into. Each respondent was asked to identify his or her ethnicity as white, black, Hispanic, Native American, Chinese, Indian, Other Asian, or Other. Furthermore, respondents were asked to name their country of citizenship while at Stanford University. The detailed information on both ethnicity and nationality, enable us to examine differences in entrepreneurial activity within the same ethnic groups across nationality status, for example, Korean Americans versus Koreans.

The survey also asks a set of questions that characterize how optimistic and positive are the respondents. In particular, it asks respondents to rate the degree to which they agree with the following statements: "I am open to new experiences," "In uncertain times, I usually expect the best," and "Overall, I expect more good things to happen to me than bad." We use these variables to control for the underlying character of the individual and to examine how optimism differs by ethnicity and nationality. Another valuable component of the survey is the information on whether the respondent's parent had entrepreneurship experience. The literature has found parental entrepreneurship status to be one of the strongest determinants of entrepreneurship in different countries. We are able to exploit the rich ethnicity and nationality information, optimism, and parental entrepreneurship status to examine how entrepreneurship differs by different ethnic and nationality groups.

Stanford University alumni and Silicon Valley entrepreneurship

Although Stanford University graduates do not represent the national population, examining the entrepreneurial activities of Stanford alumni is valuable given the important role they play in Silicon Valley entrepreneurship and high-tech entrepreneurship in general. Many Stanford alumni maintain their ties to the Bay Area and California. Forty percent of Stanford students find jobs through some form of networking, and the men and women who lead Silicon Valley's most innovative companies interact regularly by visiting campus to lecture, collaborate with faculty, and share ideas with the next generation of entrepreneurs currently filling classrooms. According to the survey an estimated 18,000 firms created by alumni are headquartered in California, generating annual worldwide sales of about $1.27 trillion and employing more than three million people. Among those who graduated after 1990, 25 percent of the responding entrepreneurs formed their companies within 20 miles of the university. For engineers whose companies populate Silicon Valley, that figure rises to 31 percent. Thirty-nine percent of all alumni-founded firms are located within 60 miles of Stanford, or roughly a one hour's drive. Five percent (2,600) of graduate students from outside the USA stayed in the Bay Area and contributed to the region's robust infrastructure and entrepreneurial spirit. Since 1984, almost 44 percent (17,265) of Stanford's graduate students have come from outside the USA. That percentage has increased in recent years to 56 percent in 2010.

Empirical approach

The empirical analysis in this chapter focuses on descriptively documenting the patterns of entrepreneurship among Asian Stanford alumni. We first examine the data to see if there are some notable differences across ethnicity and nationality. We then examine whether the descriptive patterns are statistically meaningful by performing simple statistical analyses. The empirical results presented in this chapter provide a descriptive understanding of group differences. We believe the empirical results on group differences will provide a foundation for future studies to further develop hypotheses regarding ethnic variation in entrepreneurship and the determinants.

We present results from a series of simple regressions that examine group differences in entrepreneurship status. The dependent variables are proxies of entrepreneurship status, and the dependent variables are the ethnicity (or nationality) of the individual, for example, whether he or she is Chinese, Indian, other Asian, white, Hispanic, black, and other. We are interested in the coefficient estimates on these ethnic groups, in particular the Asian ethnic groups. The coefficient estimates indicate whether the differences in entrepreneurial activity between ethnic groups (or nationalities) that we find in the descriptive analysis are statistically meaningful. We present results so that coefficient estimates present group differences relative to white Americans. We also examine participation in the program, measures of optimism, and parental entrepreneurship status as an outcome variable to examine differential selection by ethnicity and nationality. Finally, we examine whether optimism, parental entrepreneurship, and participation in the Stanford University entrepreneurship programs alters the difference in entrepreneurship by ethnicity and nationality.

Entrepreneurship patterns of Asian Stanford alumni

We first visually examine descriptive patterns of entrepreneurship to see if there are some notable differences across ethnicity and nationality. Figure 8.1 presents the share of Stanford alumni that found a new organization by ethnicity. Asians

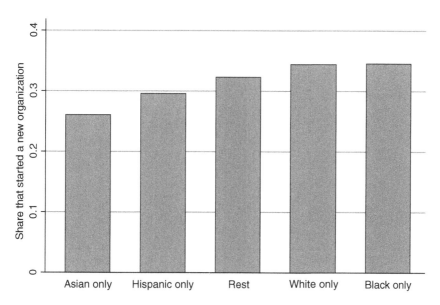

Figure 8.1 Entrepreneurship by ethnicity.

have the lowest rate of entrepreneurship followed by Hispanics. Whites and blacks have the highest rate, with over 35 percent having some entrepreneurship experience. In Figure 8.2 we subdivide the Asian ethnicity category into Chinese, Indian, and other Asian. There is a wide discrepancy in entrepreneurship across the Asian ethnicities. Other Asians have the lowest rate at slightly over 20 percent and Indians have the highest rate at over 30 percent. We note that in Figures 8.1 and 8.2 both US citizens and foreigners are included in each ethnic group.

Figure 8.3 examines the entrepreneurship rate by nationality, with a focus on Asian countries. Relative to the Americans, East Asians have the lowest rate of entrepreneurship, with Japanese below 20 percent and Chinese and Korean slightly above 20 percent. The rate of entrepreneurship among Indians is high at above 30 percent and similar to that of US citizens. Figure 8.4 compares the types of entrepreneurship, that is, whether the respondent found an incorporated company, unincorporated business, partnership, or informal business. Unincorporated businesses include sole proprietorship, individual contractors, consultants, lawyers, or free-lancers. Partnerships include limited liability companies (LLCs), law firms, etc. Examples of informal businesses include selling out of your home, cleaning services, gardening services, etc. The results indicate that entrepreneurs often create more than one type of organization, but what is most notable is the concentration of entrepreneurship towards incorporated companies in Asia relative to the USA. In particular, the rate of entrepreneurship of unincorporated businesses is substantially higher in the USA compared with that

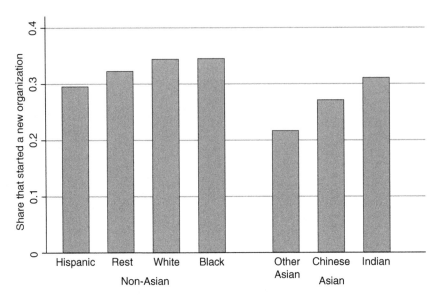

Figure 8.2 Entrepreneurship by ethnicity with Asian breakdown.

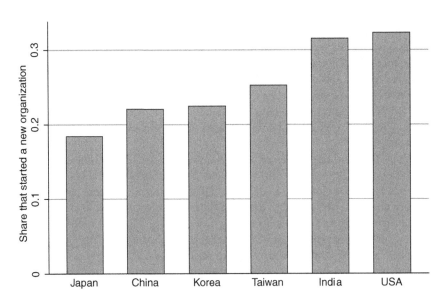

Figure 8.3 Entrepreneurship by nationality.

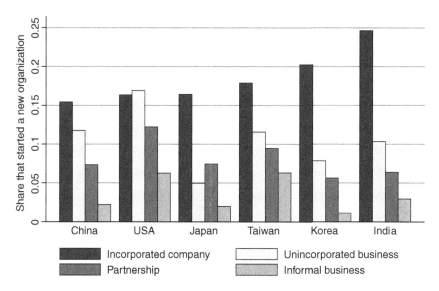

Figure 8.4 Types of entrepreneurship by nationality.

of other countries. This presents an interesting question, although one that the current chapter does not address, of whether the economic impact in terms of employment or growth is higher for Asian entrepreneurs given their focus on incorporation. Note that tech start-ups tend to incorporate rather than become an LLC for various reasons, among which include investor preference for incorporation and the suitability with stock option plans.

We then econometrically examine whether these entrepreneurship and start-up investment patterns of Stanford alumni differ statistically by ethnicity. A simple regression indicates that the share of Asians that found a new organization is about 8.4 percent lower than that of whites, and the difference is statistically significant at the 1 percent level. When we further separate the Asian category into Chinese, Indian, and other Asians, we do not find any meaningful differences in entrepreneurship between Indians or whites. However, the entrepreneurship rate for Chinese is about 7.2 percent lower than that of whites. For other Asians, incorporating about 50 percent Japanese and 22 percent Korean, entrepreneurship rate is about 13 percent points less than that of whites. However, these patterns do not separate out Asian Americans from non-American Asians. Further separating out these two groups presents an interesting picture. Table 8.1 presents the main results. Overall the table indicates that Asians of foreign nationality have substantially lower start-up rates than their Asian American counterparts. As column (1) indicates, the entrepreneurship rate among Indian Americans is not statistically distinguishable from white Americans. However, the estimates for Chinese Americans and other Asian Americans are negative and statistically significant. Chinese Americans on average have

Table 8.1 Ethnic and immigrant entrepreneurship

Variables	(1) Entrepreneurship	(2) Entrepreneurship	(3) Participate in entrepreneurship program	(4) Entrepreneurship	(5) Optimism	(6) Parental entrepreneurship	(7) Entrepreneurship	(8) Entrepreneurship
Other Asian	-0.126***	-0.126***	0.0118	-0.127***	-0.127**	-0.0467***	-0.105***	-0.105***
	(0.0194)	(0.0194)	(0.00935)	(0.0194)	(0.0640)	(0.0162)	(0.0191)	(0.0190)
Chinese	-0.0614***	-0.0614***	0.0476***	-0.0653***	-0.218***	-0.0177	-0.0442***	-0.0465***
	(0.0168)	(0.0168)	(0.00982)	(0.0168)	(0.0500)	(0.0139)	(0.0166)	(0.0166)
Indian	-0.0318	-0.0318	0.0689***	-0.0375	0.0601	-0.0264	-0.0245	-0.0279
	(0.0317)	(0.0318)	(0.0204)	(0.0318)	(0.0840)	(0.0250)	(0.0321)	(0.0321)
Other Asian *Foreign	-0.0888***							
	(0.0320)							
Other Asian *Foreign *Korean		-0.0957*	-0.0328	-0.0930*	0.150	-0.0240	-0.0987**	-0.0971**
		(0.0502)	(0.0276)	(0.0498)	(0.138)	(0.0430)	(0.0486)	(0.0484)
Other Asian *Foreign *Japanese		-0.132***	-0.0646***	-0.126***	0.0275	-0.107***	-0.112***	-0.109***
		(0.0365)	(0.0165)	(0.0365)	(0.122)	(0.0268)	(0.0354)	(0.0354)
Other Asian *Foreign *Rest		-0.00988	-0.0207	-0.00819	0.269*	0.0524	-0.0467	-0.0456
		(0.0491)	(0.0266)	(0.0491)	(0.138)	(0.0438)	(0.0460)	(0.0460)
Chinese *Foreign	-0.111***	-0.111***	-0.0440**	-0.108***	0.234***	-0.0658***	-0.111***	-0.109***
	(0.0309)	(0.0309)	(0.0183)	(0.0308)	(0.0907)	(0.0248)	(0.0302)	(0.0302)
Indian *Foreign	-0.0860*	-0.0860*	-0.0251	-0.0840*	0.235**	-0.0253	-0.0946**	-0.0933**
	(0.0470)	(0.0470)	(0.0310)	(0.0470)	(0.123)	(0.0374)	(0.0468)	(0.0468)
Participate in entrepreneurship program				0.0817***				0.0491***
				(0.0187)				(0.0183)
Optimism							0.0555***	0.0552***
							(0.00266)	(0.00266)
Parental entrepreneurship							0.216***	0.215***
							(0.00967)	(0.00968)
Observations	17,394	17,394	17,394	17,394	17,086	17,394	17,086	17,086
R-squared	0.012	0.012	0.013	0.014	0.003	0.005	0.070	0.070

Notes
Each column represents a regression and contains additional controls that include black, Hispanic, other race, black foreign, Hispanic foreign, other race foreign, and white foreign. Robust standard errors are in parentheses.
*** $p<0.01$; ** $p<0.05$; * $p<0.1$

about 6 percent lower entrepreneurship rate than white Americans, and for other Asians the rate is about 12.6 percent points lower. Moreover, what is striking is that all Asians of foreign nationality have lower start-up rates than their Asian American counterparts.

Based on the nationality information we are able to sub-divide the other Asian category into Korean, Japanese, and other Asian. Now, the other Asian category excludes Korean, Japanese, Chinese, and Indian. As column (2) indicates, the coefficient estimates on the Korean and Japanese sub-sub-groups are all negative and statistically significant. The coefficient estimate on the Japanese sub-group is quite large in magnitude at −0.13 and statistically significant at the 1 percent level. The coefficient estimates on the Korean sub-group is −0.096 and statistically significant at the 10 percent level. Even at this sub-sub-division level we find persistently lower entrepreneurship rates from students coming from Asia compared with their Asian American counterparts. We note that the results presented here are average differences by ethnicity and nationality across all alumni cohorts in the data.

Investment in start-ups is also important for the innovation ecosystem. We also examine whether one's experience as an angel investor or venture capital differs by ethnicity. Similar to the entrepreneurship results, the share of Asian Americans that become angel or VC investors are lower than whites. One unique feature of Silicon Valley venture capitalists is that many have their own start-up experiences. We examine whether entrepreneur turned investor status differs by ethnicity. Again, we find that the Asian group has a significantly lower share of entrepreneur-investors than the other ethnic categories. Overall there is consistently lower participation in start-up investment among Asians.

University entrepreneurship program participation by ethnicity and nationality

The difference between Asian Americans and Asians in entrepreneurship suggests that, despite the cultural traits shared among Asians, the experience in the USA generates large differences in start-up activity. Then a natural question is whether these differences within each Asian ethnic sub-group decrease as foreign Asian students attend US universities and take advantage of the university entrepreneurship programs. In this section we examine whether attending classes and participating in Stanford University's entrepreneurship program affects the differences in entrepreneurship activity between American and foreign Asian sub-groups. We focus on two major entrepreneurship programs initiated by Stanford University: the Center for Entrepreneurial Studies (CES) and the Stanford Technology Venture Program (STVP).

Stanford University is well known for its supportive environment for student and faculty entrepreneurship. The stories of the founding of Hewlett-Packard and Google are some of many examples. Stanford University further expanded and more formalized its support for entrepreneurship by establishing two initiatives—the CES and the STVP—in the mid-1990s. The CES was founded in 1996 at the Graduate School of Business to address the needs facing entrepreneurs and the entrepreneurial community. It is a collaborative effort that spans the whole university and supports research and teaching in a variety of ways. The CES offers a variety of courses that touch upon the various aspects of entrepreneurship from all different schools in Stanford. These courses cover topics ranging over management, finance, technology, law, education, design, etc., and are primarily accessible to the business school students. Furthermore, experiential opportunities where students can learn the day-to-day activities of a start-up or test out new business concepts are offered through the CES. The STVP is the entrepreneurship center founded in 1995 at the Engineering School. It offers courses and extracurricular programs for students, as well as supporting research on high-technology entrepreneurship. The STVP houses several fellowship programs where students can get in-depth knowledge and experience of technology start-ups, and a variety of courses are offered through the Engineering School.

Our focus here is to see whether there are differences in participation in Stanford University's entrepreneurship programs by ethnicity. Again, we're interested in whether there are differences between Asians and Asians Americans. As column (3) indicates, Chinese American and Indian American participation is significantly higher than white Americans. However, participation is lower for their Asian counterparts, especially for the Japanese and Chinese. Such pattern potentially suggests that the differential participation in entrepreneurship education could be driving the differences in start-up activity between these groups. In column (4) we additionally include entrepreneurship program participation to the base regression as a control variable. Indeed participation in these programs is associated with about 8 percent points more entrepreneurship. However, the coefficient estimates on the ethnic groups in column (4) are surprisingly similar to those in column (2). Controlling for program participation does not reduce the within Asian ethnic sub-group differences in entrepreneurship. This indicates that the differential participation in educational opportunities is not driving the difference in entrepreneurship between ethnic groups by nationality.

Optimism and parental entrepreneurship by ethnicity and nationality

We have documented the substantial differences in the entrepreneurial activities between Asian Americans and Asians. Moreover, they also differ significantly in the degree of participation in Stanford University's entrepreneurship initiatives. Why are Asians less entrepreneurial and why do they use entrepreneurship training to a lesser degree? The differences in entrepreneurship based on ethnicity and nationality suggest that there could be differences in important characteristics that determine start-up activity. In this section, we examine whether the two known determinants of entrepreneurship, optimism and parental entrepreneurship, differ by ethnicity and nationality.

One widely examined individual characteristic among entrepreneurship scholars is optimism. People who tend to have positive viewpoints and are optimistic play down the potential negative consequences when start-ups fail. Also, more optimistic people tend to overestimate the returns to entrepreneurship and are more likely to enter into entrepreneurship. In this regard, we examine whether optimism differs by ethnicity and whether such difference can explain the difference in entrepreneurship across ethnicities. We construct a measure of optimism based on the responses to whether one is more open to new experiences, expects the best in uncertain times, and overall expects more good things to happen than bad things. Column (5) indicates that East Asian Americans generally have lower levels of optimism compared with white Americans. However, their Asian counterparts tend to be more optimistic than their Asian American counterparts. There is no statistical difference in optimism between Asian Americans and non-American Asians of Korean or Japanese ancestry. Given that columns (1) and (2) indicate that Asians have lower entrepreneurship rate than their Asian American counterparts, it seems unlikely that optimism is driving the difference in entrepreneurship by ethnicity.

Next, we turn to parental entrepreneurship status in column (6). Asian Americans are less likely to have a parent with entrepreneurship experience than white Americans. The effect is strongest for the other Asian Americans. Furthermore, Asians are less likely than Asian Americans to have a parent with entrepreneurship experience. Further sub-dividing the other Asian category reveals that the negative difference holds for most nationalities and is statistically strongest for the Japanese and Chinese. Parental entrepreneurship is lower among Asian Americans and even more so for East Asians. As parental entrepreneurship status is one of the strongest and most persistent predictors of entrepreneurship, the low parental entrepreneurship rate among East Asians could present a hurdle in promoting entrepreneurship in their respective homelands.

In the next column, we examine whether controlling for optimism and parental entrepreneurship can reduce the group differences in entrepreneurship. As expected, optimism and parental entrepreneurship are both strong predictors of entrepreneurship. However, controlling for those two variables in the regression does little to alter the ethnic differences in entrepreneurship among Asians and Asian Americans. Finally, in the last column we control for optimism, parental entrepreneurship status, and participation in entrepreneurship education programs. The coefficient estimates on the ethnic groups barely change. Overall, the results indicate that there is surprisingly strong persistence in the differences in entrepreneurship among Asians and Asian Americans, which cannot be explained away with traditional determinants of entrepreneurship. The stark difference in entrepreneurship between Asian Americans and Asians among Stanford University alumni suggests that despite the cultural traits shared within each Asian sub-group, the difference in institutional and educational upbringing in the USA can generate large differences in start-up activity.

Conclusion

This chapter examined the entrepreneurship patterns of Asians and Asian Americans. We find that among Stanford alumni, Asians have a substantially lower start-up rate than Asian Americans. Such discrepancy not only holds for entrepreneurial choice but also for investing as an angel investor or VC, or becoming an entrepreneur investor. There are significant differences in the participation in Stanford University's entrepreneurship program between ethnic groups. Asians have lower participation rates in Stanford University's entrepreneurship education program, compared with their Asian American counterparts. However, we find that participating in these programs as a student does little to reduce the gap in entrepreneurship among ethnic groups. Optimism and parental entrepreneurship status are strong predictors of entrepreneurship. Optimism is low for Asian Americans but high for Asians. On the other hand, parental entrepreneurship is lower among Asians. However, controlling for both optimism and parental entrepreneurship again does little to reduce the gap in entrepreneurship rates.

Lee and Eesley (2017) examine the intergenerational persistence in entrepreneurship, that is, a correlation between one's entrepreneurship status and one's parents' entrepreneurship status by ethnicity. They find that the intergenerational correlation of entrepreneurship is quite high for East Asians compared with US citizens. In other words, conditional on one's parent being an entrepreneur, the probability of the child becoming an entrepreneur is higher in East Asia. The flipside is that if one does not have an entrepreneur parent, one is significantly less likely to become an entrepreneur in East Asia. The low level of parental entrepreneurship and the high degree of intergenerational correlation in entrepreneurship among East Asians likely result in the lower level of entrepreneurship and interest in university entrepreneurship programs among Asians relative to their Asian American counterparts.

The difference in entrepreneurship between Asian Americans and Asians potentially points to the importance of immigration policy in fostering entrepreneurship. Young Asian immigrants who grow up in the USA are much more entrepreneurial than Asian foreign students with little experience in US society, despite similar educational credentials. Allowing immigrants to settle in and attain the cultural and institutional features of the US education system positively influences entrepreneurship and innovation, at least among the skilled population. Our findings highlight the value of immigration in terms of breaking the persistence in entrepreneurship among Asians and promoting potential high-growth entrepreneurship in the USA. In addition, incorporating Asian American entrepreneurs within Asian countries to promote entrepreneurship may help break the persistence of entrepreneurship in Asia.

Finally, the results present a sobering picture for Asian countries that are currently pursuing various policies to promote entrepreneurship and innovation. The low levels of parental entrepreneurship highlight the underlying socio-economic constraints in entrepreneurship. The high intergenerational persistence in entrepreneurship further hinders younger Asians to break away from the low equilibrium. In some aspects, the entrepreneurial push pursued by Asian governments is needed to break away from the spiral of low entrepreneurship and the high intergenerational persistence in entrepreneurship. However, the significant difference in entrepreneurial activities we find between Asian Americans and Asians may provide another way to promote entrepreneurship in Asia. Asian Americans often inherit the language and cultural backgrounds from their parents and are better able to integrate within their native land, enabling them to navigate through the bureaucracies and culture of Asia while supplying innovative business ideas. Policies that promote such transnational bridging may indeed serve as an effective yet low cost way to promote entrepreneurship (Shin and Choi 2015).

References

Adelino, Manuel, Antoinette Schoar, and Felipe Severino. 2015. "House Prices, Collateral, and Self-Employment." Journal of Financial Economics 117(2): 288–306.

Aldrich, Howard E. and Catherinze Zimmer. 1986. "Entrepreneurship Through Social Networks." In The Art and Science of Entrepreneurship, eds. Donald Sexton and Raymond Smilor. New York: Ballinger, 3–23.

Aldrich, Howard E. and Roger Waldinger. 1990. "Ethnicity and Entrepreneurship." Annual Review of Sociology 16: 1–327.

Alesina, Alberto, and Paola Giuliano. 2013. Culture and Institutions. Cambridge, Mass.: National Bureau of Economic Research.

Bertrand, Marianne and Antoinette Schoar. 2006. "The Role of Family in Firms." Journal of Economic Perspectives 20(2): 73–96.

Fairlie, Robert W. 1999. "The Absence of the African-American Owned Business: An Analysis of the Dynamics of Self-Employment." Journal of Labor Economics 17(1): 80–108.

Fairlie, Robert W., and Alicia M. Robb. 2007. "Why are Black-Owned Businesses Less Successful than White-Owned Businesses? The Role of Families, Inheritances, and Business Human Capital." Journal of Labor Economics.

Fernandez, Raquel. 2010. "Does Culture Matter?" Cambridge, Mass.: National Bureau of Economic Research.

Guiso, Luigi, Paola Sapienza, and Luigi Zingales. 2004. "Does Culture Affect Economic Outcomes?" Journal of Economic Perspectives: 23–48.

Kerr, William R., and Martin Mandorff. 2015. "Social Networks, Ethnicity, and Entrepreneurship." NBER Working Paper No. 21597.

Kerr, William R. and Ramana Nanda. 2009. "Democratizing entry: Banking deregulations, financing constraints, and entrepreneurship." Journal of Financial Economics 94(1), 124–149.

Lee, Yong Suk and Chuck Eesley. 2018. "The persistence of entrepreneurship and innovative immigrants." Research Policy. In press.

Lerner, Josh, and Ulrike Malmendier. 2013. "With a Little Help from My (Random) Friends: Success and Failure in Post-Business School Entrepreneurship." Review of Financial Studies 26(10): 2411–2452.

Samila, Sampsa and Olav Sorensen. 2011. "Venture capital, entrepreneurship, and economic growth." The Review of Economics and Statistics 93(1): 338–349.

Saxenian, AnnaLee. 2006. The New Argonauts: Regional Advantage in a Global Economy, Cambridge: Harvard Univ. Press.

Saxenian, AnnaLee. 1999. Silicon Valley's New Immigrant Entrepreneurs. San Francisco: Public Policy Institute of California.

Shin, Gi-Wook and Joon Nak Choi. 2015. Global talent: Skilled labor as social capital in Korea. Stanford University Press.

9 Bridging and the success of Korean firms in China

An entrepreneurial understanding

Joon-Shik Park

This chapter examines how the *chaebol* and their expatriate managers managed risks when entering the Chinese market, focusing on the large manufacturing firms (e.g., Samsung, LG, and Hyundai-Kia) and their key suppliers—firms that are leading Korean-style globalization in China. My core contention is that the success of the *chaebol* in leveraging ethnic Koreans in China (the Korean Chinese) demonstrates that some of the strategic and operational problems raised in Chapters 2 through 5 in this volume can be alleviated by leveraging diverse and inclusive social networks, as called for by Chapters 6, 7, and 8. Although China posed unparalleled market opportunities for the *chaebol*, it nevertheless posed unique risks. Leading Korean manufacturers, which had experience in leveraging informal social ties to succeed in a Korea where the pace of economic development outstripped formal rules and institutions, quickly recognized the potential for the Korean Chinese to bridge cultural, institutional, and social divides. The Korean Chinese functioned as transnational bridges (Shin and Choi 2015), linking the *chaebol* with the Chinese environment and reducing transaction costs for the *chaebol*. These individuals translated culturally contingent nuances between Korean and Chinese cultures, educated Korean managers about the Chinese environment, and facilitated cooperation between *chaebol* and their local partners. The Korean Chinese played an especially important role in building political ties between the *chaebol* and state and party officials, which was crucial given the tremendous influence wielded by officials in the Chinese economy. The nexus between the Korean Chinese and the *chaebol* has been mutually beneficial, and has contributed towards a new multiculturalism within the *chaebol* and in Korean and Chinese societies at large, fostering diversity within the context of *jus sanguinis* Korean national identity.

The *chaebol* in China

During the last three decades, China has emerged as the pivotal political and economic force in Asia. The speed and magnitude of the rise of China has made it a potentially lucrative market for foreign firms. Korea has been no exception, and has leveraged growing Chinese consumption power. Since Korea opened official diplomatic relations with China in 1992, China has emerged as Korea's biggest trading partner; from 1992 to 2012, trade between two countries has increased 34.6 times, and now surpasses Korea's trade with the USA and Japan combined. For this reason, it is no exaggeration to say that business relations with China have become an essential element for sustaining the Korean economy. Indeed, there is a widespread consensus that the integration of China into the global economy has been an important factor for Korean globalization in the recent past (Ito and Hahn 2010; SERI 2004), although Chinese firms have now emerged as legitimate rivals to Korean rivals (see Chapters 1 and 2 in this volume).

During the 1992–2012 period, China became the most important investment destination of Korean firms for two reasons. First, China became a production base for Korean firms, enabling the *chaebol* to leverage lower wages and other costs to generate a cost advantage in world markets. Second, China also became an important market for Korean consumer products. While industrial firms like Samsung and Hyundai have historically recorded high sales in China, perhaps in no other sector have Korean firms succeeded as spectacularly in China as in cultural products. The cultural phenomena called *hallryu* or the "Korean Wave," encompassing pop music, dramas, and other forms of entertainment, not only directly benefited firms in the cultural industries, but also contributed greatly towards the popularity of Korean products among Chinese consumers. Furthermore, as the consumption power of the Chinese has grown, they have begun to visit Korea on a massive scale, generating windfall profits among hotels, department stores, resorts, shopping malls, and even property developers in major Korean cities and travel destinations. Within a short period, Chinese visitors have become the leading customer for Korean retail and tourism-related businesses. Overall, China has provided decisive momentum for Korean globalization, as the *chaebol* have made massive investment in China and as China has become a leading marketplace for Korean goods.

Despite its potential, the Chinese market has been notoriously difficult for foreign firms to successfully penetrate. Risks can be found at three distinct levels of analysis: political-systemic, administrative-bureaucratic, and managerial-operational (Shin-Huang 2014). Political and economic risks relate to China's aggressive foreign policies and its opaque and underdeveloped institutions. Administrative-bureaucratic risks relate to central, provincial, or local government policies affecting the trade, investment, and employment decisions of foreign firms. Managerial-operational risks often relate to the need to manage their local human resources, supply chains, and social relationships in general. My core contention in this chapter is that the *chaebol* have leveraged the skills and social networks of the Korean Chinese to manage these risks effectively.

To investigate this proposition, this chapter relies on seven in-depth interviews of long-serving Korean expatriates who had worked for various *chaebol* or their major suppliers in China. The interviews were conducted during two waves (in 2002 and 2011), when I visited the Chinese regional headquarters and factories for *chaebol* and crucial Korean suppliers operating in China; the interview locations were spread throughout China, including Beijing, Suzhou, and

Huizhou. The interviews themselves were designed to probe the viewpoints that expatriate managers held, in addition to their viewpoints and practices regarding important strategic and operational issues. Towards this end, I used ethnographic interviews where I asked expatriate managers to describe their daily lives and activities in China and their opinions and perspectives on their rival East Asian multinational manufacturers in their own words, noting that most Korean manufacturers in China were competing against manufacturers from Taiwan or Japan. Interview and conversation topics generally covered four broad areas, including their careers, family lives, important tasks, and future expectations. We also raised operational issues such as their relationship with the Chinese employees and their superiors in Korea, human resource policies in China and the management of administrative and bureaucratic relations with the Chinese government. Finally, we asked about broad strategic issues such as the opportunities and risks posed by China, including political and systematic risks. Interviews were about two hours each on average. To supplement these interviews with corporate managers, I also conducted in-depth discussions with former China experts.

The growth of China and the rise of new challenges

The entry of Korean business groups into China

The *chaebol* began to make substantial investments in China during the early 2000s, more than a decade later than their Japanese counterparts; however, they were able to catch up to and surpass their Japanese competitors because they acted very aggressively once they decided to become major players in China. Korean FDI into China almost tripled from 2001 to 2004, increasing from US$2.2 billion to US$6.2 billion.[1] A former Samsung executive based in its China headquarters in Beijing described this process as follows:

> I served in China for most of my career at Samsung. When I started working at the Beijing office, we were busy gathering information on Japanese companies' activities in China, because they started much earlier in China [than us]. We tried to bring in retired Japanese managers who had China experience and their advice and consultation were one of the ways we could get business information from on Chinese market. Japanese advice and information were very helpful in getting into China business early on. However, our reliance on Japanese experience quickly ended and we decided to launch massive investments in China. [translated from Korean]

Major Korean manufacturers in particular regarded China as a strategic location for production and sales. As latecomers, they tried to catch up with rivals as fast as possible. *Chaebol* such as Samsung, LG, Hyundai-Kia, and SK moved major manufacturing clusters into China. Indeed, China now accounts for the largest share of overseas investments of fixed assets by Samsung Electronics, more than that of the USA and Japan. Hyundai-Kia also expanded their production capacities in China as fast as possible, and won the second biggest market share in China among multinational producers in 2013. A former Hyundai Beijing executive described Hyundai-Kia's growth in China as follows:

> China is an indispensable part of Hyundai's strategy. The fast growth of Hyundai-Kia motors has been accompanied by their swarm of Korean partner companies. We have been trying to move in China not as a stand-alone company but as a family of closely related companies. Leaving China is unthinkable, because Hyundai-Kia has already placed too many assets in China. Hyundai-Kia has grown in China into the third largest foreign car manufacturer and wants to remain as a leading auto maker in China. The success of Hyundai is the result of its speed and investment timing. We were able to build faster than competitors and engaged much more aggressively wherever market opportunities emerged. Such risk-friendliness may explain the fast rise of Hyundai-Kia manufacturing in China. [translated from Korean]

Worth noting is that Samsung and Hyundai built their largest office buildings in China, indicating that their operations in China were not limited to manufacturing but also included more sophisticated business activities. According to former China managers, the *chaebol*s' China headquarters in Beijing have become the most important Asian centers, replacing the position of their Japan headquarters in Tokyo. A former manager at Samsung's Beijing headquarters explained the position of China in Samsung:

> I have been working as a China manager for about 20 years. I started my overseas manager career in Hong Kong. At that time, the Hong Kong office was gathering information about China. Samsung was very cautious even after the normalization of Korea-China relations, and closely observed the China market. However, their decision to invest in China started after they barely recovered from the [so-called] IMF crisis [i.e., the Asian Financial Crisis] in the late 1990s. After Samsung decided to build factories in China, it quickly started manufacturing in China and expanded very fast. At first, China was regarded as a manufacturing outpost for Samsung. However, the China market became more and more important. With the growth of China, Samsung began to work to establish a permanent business center in Beijing. Now, Beijing has become the regional center in our China business, encompassing other production centers scattered around China. As China business expanded, the status of Beijing clearly eclipsed that of Tokyo. It has now grown into the Asian center. [translated from Korean]

The localization of Korean business groups in China

Localization, or adaptation to a foreign environment by adopting local practices, building local connections, and hiring local managers, is among the most effective approaches to succeeding in foreign markets. Most of the *chaebol* understood and emphasized the necessity of localization. For instance, Samsung and many Korean companies are intentionally portraying themselves as global companies, wanting to balance their identities as Korean and global companies. Samsung never portrays itself as a Korean multinational; rather, it always emphasizes how it is a leading global company, even though Samsung was founded in Korea and matured there, according to one Samsung Beijing headquarter manager.

The limited strategic leverage possessed by the *chaebol* pushed them towards greater localization. Having placed too much of a bet on China to consider retreating from the Chinese market, the *chaebol* understand their limited strategic freedom and flexibility. Now, their only realistic option is to hedge their risks by adapting to China through localization or 'Chinization.' One of the best examples of this approach is Hyundai-Kia in China, which was able to become the fifth largest automobile producer in the world because of its success in China. Indeed, its production volume in China nearly matches its volume in Korea. Without China, Hyundai-Kia would not match its global competitors in scale, and the company clearly understands its dependence on the China market.

Rather than asking the Chinese to meet them halfway, the *chaebol* adapted to Chinese approaches and practices. One advantage that the *chaebol* have had is that they are more comfortable with informal agreements based on social relationships than their Western or Japanese rivals, which rely much more on formal agreements and the rule of law. Having matured in Korea during its own rapid development, the *chaebol* have imprinted upon an environment where transparency, formal contracts, and the rule of law were not well established. In that sense, the Chinese market was not altogether different from the Korean market through the 1990s. Korean big business has adapted to strong market discipline while maintaining ties with the state. The idea of augmenting market competition with the visible hand of the state remains embedded into the habits of Korean big businesses, and this has worked well in China. Overall, the *chaebol* have embodied a mix of informalism and the market-driven formalism of the West (see Chapter 3 of this volume for details), and found themselves well-positioned to grow rapidly in China.

The construction and maintenance of *guanxi* networks has been a crucial element of Korean firms' success in China. *Guanxi*—social relationships of reciprocal exchange—are considered extremely important in China. In particular, *guanxi* with state and party officials enable firms to lobby for favorable regulations and access to state-controlled resources, among many other benefits (Peng and Luo 2000). With regard to *guanxi*, Korean firms have been very aggressive, as they have long regarded good social networks as important to their business success. As discussed in Chapters 2 and 3 of this volume, a culture of strict hierarchy, uniform control, and close ties between powerful business interests and the state were deeply embedded in Korean firms. Given this experience, Korean expatriate managers regarded taking care of key social ties between their business and their Chinese partners as one of the most important roles of their everyday lives. This management culture, which emphasizes *guanxi* networks, is one of the factors that differentiates the approach Korean firms have taken in China from their Japanese competitors. Every Korean manager working at LG and Samsung factories in China whom we interviewed explained that an important part of their work went beyond maintenance and production within their factories, which their Japanese counterparts focused upon. Instead, they also play a social role connecting the firm with Chinese local authorities and employees. One Korean expatriate ostensibly focusing on managing production and technical issues described the importance of *guanxi* in his job:

> I feel not much difference between China and Korea in terms of relating to people. Compared with Japanese managers, we have been very active in terms of getting along with Chinese employees. My company also expects me to expand my social networks with Chinese local authorities. Whenever my superior visits our China factory, I have to connect them to Chinese authorities, and management of human relations is one of the important jobs of Korean expatriates. Even though my background is that of a production manager and technician, I have to handle other jobs like human management. I always feel some pressure to have good human relations and maintain information sources.

Even though Korean companies could not establish strong institutional systems and multicultural human resource management as their global competitors did, they tried to compensate for their weakness by taking advantage of their knowledge of Asian business culture and skill in social networking. Of course, *guanxi* has exposed Korean firms to political risk, making them sensitive to power competition between political figures in China. However, those risks have not caused many problems for Korean firms to date, which may indirectly indicate that their business practices are working in China.

Korean multiculturalism, new loops of human circulation and localization

The remarkable success of this strategy cannot be explained without recognizing the role of ethnic Koreans in China. Korean firms and expatriates have had a profound impact on ethnic Korean communities in China, as the investment and massive presence of Korean companies and their employees created new opportunities for ethnic Koreans. Korean Chinese parents had long been willing to invest in the education of their children, to open better economic opportunities in Beijing, Japan, and Korea. During the last two decades, about 1 million ethnic Koreans left their rural communities to find new jobs and build economic ties, many with Korean firms across both China and Korea. Compared with more advanced rivals, Korean firms faced real constraints in constructing and managing multicultural environments in their workplaces (see Chapter 3 in this volume for details). Yet, the *chaebol* were able to compensate for their weaknesses by constructing a uniquely diverse environment within the Korean cultural context in China.

The *chaebol* and their suppliers created several key advantages by leveraging the Korean diaspora. Ethnic Koreans have long been more than cheap labor for Korean manufacturers, and have engaged in a wide range of activities including marketing, management, negotiation, and businesses development. These Korean Chinese had tacit knowledge and social capital relevant to the Chinese market, and had much to offer Korean firms with whom they were linked through common bonds of kinship, language, and culture. Ethnic Koreans were well-integrated into Chinese society while retaining a Korean identity, and embodied the kind of transnationalism that would enable them to function across both societies (see Shin and Choi 2015 for a full explication of the transnational bridging argument). Having a dual identity with Korean and Chinese elements was part of their cultural repertoire, so that most Korean Chinese felt that they could naturally work for both Korea and China. Indeed, the ethnic Koreans whom we met in the Chinese factories and offices of Korean firms were working to be recognized and rewarded as corporate citizens of Korean firms while simultaneously retaining a Chinese national identity. One Korean Chinese Samsung manager described this experience:

> I was born in Yeonbyun, a remote and [majority] ethnic Korean town in Northern China, and graduated from the local university. I was lucky because I was able to join Samsung when the company needed a Chinese translator in its Suzhou factory. I worked to connect Korean managers with local employees and the company promoted me fast. I found a better apartment for my family and was motivated to work even harder for the company, because I saw opportunities as a manager who understood both Chinese and Korean businessmen. However, I still think of myself as a Chinese citizen and want to maintain this. [translated from Korean]

Korean firms instantly noticed the potential usefulness of ethnic Koreans in China as valuable assets who facilitated the smooth landing of Korean firms into China and provided networks with the Chinese market. Brokerage, negotiation, and communication skills are core skills for global business, making global companies compete to attract the talents of those who can bridge different societies in a phenomenon that has become known as "the global war for talent." Finding and recruiting brokers, instead of spending time and money training individuals to develop these skills and cultural repertoires, was an instant advantage for the *chaebol* and their suppliers, as they could leverage cheap and highly qualified Korean Chinese. Leveraging this advantage, the *chaebol* and their suppliers regarded the Korean Chinese as "human brokers" to bridge Korea and China. Having a strong understanding of both Korean culture and the Chinese context, ethnic Koreans were well positioned to translate culturally specific nuances across the two contexts and to facilitate cooperation between them, beyond helping Korean managers understand the Chinese market and target consumers there. Understanding this, many Korean firms aggressively hired ethnic Koreans, and took advantage of ethnic Koreans' human and social capital during their initial entry into China (Sonoda et al. 2014). Indeed, the best example of the contribution that the Korean Chinese made to Korean firms was perhaps the *guanxi* that they established, as Korean firms depended especially heavily on their ethnic Korean employees in the early stages of their entry into China to build up *guanxi* networks. This has generated tangible and substantial strategic advantages for Korean firms, as the ability to link China-specific knowledge and embedded know-how with Korean business processes has become a defining characteristic of Korean businesses in China.

This capability has enabled Korean firms to expand their operations into industries such as retailing, consumer products, and cultural products, which have largely been challenging to other foreign companies. China has become increasingly challenging for foreign consumer brands, with the exception of luxury goods, product categories introduced into China by foreign brands (e.g., coffee), and others (e.g., baby formula) where Chinese brands were no longer trusted after major scandals (Bain and Kantar Worldpanel 2014). Unlike manufacturing, where product features were standardized across countries to a substantial degree, consumer goods businesses needed to customize their products to local consumers. For the purpose of understanding local Chinese consumers, leveraging ethnic Koreans has been crucial, as social and cultural knowledge was the key to success. To date, Korean firms have been successful in consumer goods segments that no other foreign firms have penetrated, such as mass-market cosmetics.

It is worth noting that the relationship between Korean firms and Korean Chinese communities in China has been mutually beneficial. Korean firms provided invaluable economic opportunities and contributed towards rising socio-economic conditions. During the last two decades, the majority of young ethnic Koreans left rural communities to find jobs in Korean firms in China or pursue economic opportunities in Korea itself. This migration has transformed their communities, as ethnic Koreans in China were drawn into Korean firms and Korea itself. Today, about 0.7 million Chinese citizens are residing in Korea, and among them, over 0.4 million ethnic Koreans. As a result, a multicultural mix has emerged in some Korean urban areas, combining Korean and Chinese elements as symbolic icons of the growing Chinese presence. Human mobility and business activities are rapidly transforming urban landscapes in Korea. For instance, the Garibong-dong district in Seoul features a Little China today, and is an excellent example of East Asian regionalization. The urban mixture of ethnic Koreans, Korean Chinese, and North Korean refugees has revitalized a declining neighborhood in post-industrial Seoul, although the multicultural mix has created new conflicts among the groups living there.[2] Even though the role of ethnic Koreans in China has sometimes been controversial, they have undeniably reshaped their life courses through the enormous economic opportunities in bridging Korea and China. Once living in well-defined ethnic Korean communities in Manchuria such as Yeonbyeon and Gillym, ethnic Koreans with Chinese citizenship are now prospering in urban, multicultural spaces in Seoul.

Overall, there have been major synergies between Korean firms and ethnic Koreans in China, especially during their initial stages of Korean firms' entry into China. They not only provided Korean companies with significant human capital advantages compared with their Japanese competitors, but also with social capital advantages, as bridges between Korean managers and Chinese partners. As explorers of an expanding market in China, they provided Korean firms with essential ingredients for successful localization. Some ethnic Koreans working for Korean firms have been very successful, and a few of them have even become the heads of Korean firms' subsidiaries in China. Beyond their role in bridging Korean firms and Chinese society, the Korean Chinese are now expanding their transnational activities across other business areas, including services, culture, education, and tourism.

In many *chaebol* today, the role of ethnic Koreans is increasingly being filled by ethnic Chinese employees or the new generation of Koreans trained as China experts, although many SMEs are continuing to rely on the Korean Chinese. Although China emerged as a driving force for multiculturalism in Korea, there remain doubts whether the *chaebol* could really embrace multiculturalism. Indeed, many Korean firms continue to prefer Korean citizens of Korean ethnicity, who fit more easily into the homogeneous environments found in most Korean firms (see Chapter 3 for a description of these environments). Furthermore, even those Korean firms that would prefer to shift towards multiculturalism are facing difficulties in maintaining their foreign human resources; compared with other multinationals from the USA or Japan, Korean firms have not been sufficiently attractive to attract the most talented Chinese human capital. Regardless, it is clear that ethnic Koreans reduced the enormous transaction costs associated with entry into the Chinese market by lubricating social frictions and reducing learning costs, which might have been a heavy burden in the absence of ethnic Koreans in China.

The rise of Korean experts on China

Beyond the Korean Chinese, the *chaebol* have also been developing their Korean employees into China experts. These firms have strongly incentivized core expatriates in China to localize; for instance, to develop careers managing the firm's Chinese subsidiary, managers are required to have localized language, social, and managerial skills in addition to technical abilities. As the companies try to diversify their activities, their recruiting efforts are now expanding into the training of university students. More and more young students and candidates including Korean as well as local students are attracted to universities in Korea and China to have job opportunities to be future China managers. Companies are investing much into an army of China experts and have taken a long-term perspective, which indicates that they want to be treated as important players in China (Sonoda et al. 2014).

The *chaebol* built up their pools of China experts relatively quickly. Up to the 1990s, the international activities of Korean firms were mostly confined to the USA, Japan, and the European Union. The remarkable growth of China and the subsequent entry of Korean firms into China, however, caused demand for professionals working as permanent expatriate employees to skyrocket, and universities in Korea initiated Chinese language, culture, and management programs. China-oriented firms themselves also built in-house training programs, starting with intensive training in the Chinese language spanning two to six months and also in culture and business conditions, engaging Korean Chinese employees as teachers. The Korean way of training Chinese experts has been a "generalist" model, meaning that China experts must be equipped with specialized expertise as well as a general management ability; their emphasis on language and human skills in addition to technical expertise may be the consequences of their human resources strategy of internal development (see Chapter 3 in this volume for details). Only trained managers who acquired language competency were dispatched to China for sojourns averaging about five years. During these sojourns, firms usually provided their employees generous support for maintaining their families in China. The growth potential and importance of China later provided managers more opportunities to develop their careers, creating a positive feedback loop between motivation, training, and support. Those activities, which occurred rapidly, enabled a vast expansion of Korean business networks throughout major Chinese cities and industrial districts within a decade. Increasingly, there has been a new generation of China experts, trained at top universities both in Korea and China.

Samsung is widely known for its global experts program. Since the early 1990s Samsung has selected young employees to become future overseas managers and sent them abroad for about five years each to become experts on specific overseas regions. When the program started, it drew attention because Samsung asked individuals for nothing beyond a willingness to become a global expert. Its program was notable given its long-term perspective and investment horizon. While many Korean companies including Samsung continue to be criticized for a deficiency in their globalization, they have nevertheless been serious in their education and systematic training of a veritable army of global managers. Samsung required its China experts to be fluent in local languages and expected them to take charge of the overall management of its local businesses. Many of those global experts are now leading Samsung's businesses in their respective regions.[3] One manager whom we interviewed related his experience in this program:

> I started my career as an engineer at Samsung. When I heard that Samsung was trying to train China experts, I decided to step up to the challenge. Fortunately, I was selected as a young global manager who had the potential to grow into a China expert. I soon learned Chinese, undergoing a short but intensive company language program. Samsung's human resource development center offers a very intensive and strict language education. People

need to pass the company's high standard to be chosen as a regional specialist. I have been working for Samsung's China factory for more than five years and hope to return to Korea to be promoted into more challenging positions. My experience in China will help me, because the Chinese market is growing very fast and there will be more and more challenging jobs in the future.

China-oriented training programs and sojourns provided an upwardly mobile career track for managers. The *chaebol* wanted to maintain a small number of core expatriates as general production managers. As time goes on after entry, however, the number of expatriates has tended to decrease while most mundane management tasks were delegated to local managers. Professional managers who will remain as China experts are expected to accumulate communication skills, professional knowledge about production and human resources management. Afterwards, they hope to be promoted into higher level regional manager roles.

Conclusion

During the last two decades, Korea has been able to leverage China's growth. China has provided an economic frontier for Korean firms. Indeed, the *chaebol* have become global companies by taking advantage of China opportunities. The mutual interdependence of China and Korea started from direct manufacturing investment. The growth of China and globalization of Korean conglomerates reinforced each other, reinforcing mutual economic interdependence. It is undeniable that China has provided remarkable economic benefits for Korea (Moon 2010; Lee Kwang-Jae 2012; Lim Hyun-Jin and Lim Hae-Ran 2013; Jung Jae-Ho 2011), although China has increasingly become a competitor as well (see Chapters 1 and 2 of this volume).

Compared with other East Asian countries, Korean firms were much less risk adverse of the emergence of China, and were able to take maximum advantage of the China opportunity. Expansion of human and economic exchanges with China is widely regarded as the cornerstone for the sustainable growth in China of leading Korean firms. Although Korean firms' ability to manage political connections proved inadequate when Korean and Chinese national interests came into conflict, for instance during 2017 regarding Korea's installation of the American THAAD missile defense system, this ability has nevertheless proved instrumental for Korean firms' broader success in China.

In building their networks, Korean firms took advantage of ethnic Koreans. Korean multinationals arrived in China later than Japanese and Western competitors, and had few technological advantages. However, they were very successful in taking significant market share, through responsiveness to the local environment as well as their speed and agility (see Chapter 3 in this volume). More than one million ethnic Koreans in China provided them with human and social capital, functioning as bridges, social connections, and cultural assimilators absent in Japanese and Western companies. Even though Korean multinationals were not as mature as to be global, multicultural workplaces, they were success-ful in taking advantage of ethnic social capital. Korean companies were able to enjoy the China-specific social capital provided by ethnic Korean communities in China.

The positive economic reinforcement between the ethnic Korean community and Korean firms has been continuing to date. Korean firms provided ethnic Koreans rare opportunities to advance into the Chinese middle class, while gaining invaluable trust, bridging, cultural affinity, and brokerage benefits. Such a Korean style of business multiculturalism and enhanced diversity seems to be one of the elements of the transnational social capital behind the growth of Korean firms in China. The circulation and interpenetration among Korean com-munities in China and Korea may evolve into a form of multicultural social capital circulating transnational Korean talents between Korea and China (Shin and Choi 2015).

While my findings highlight the salience of the diversity discussed in the latter half of this edited volume as a solution to the strategic and operational problems discussed in the earlier half, they are subject to numerous limitations. First, there has been a difference in outcomes between the *chaebol* and SMEs. The *chaebol* have had the resources to invest in China long term, without having to worry too much about their immediate performances. They are enjoying more favorable treatment from the Chinese government, as they are large enough to have some bargaining power vis-à-vis the Chinese government. In contrast, SMEs have had to worry more about day-to-day survival, having fewer resources and barely remaining operational in many cases, echoing themes raised in Chapter 4. Thus, they have had to be far more cost-conscious over the short term. Many SMEs were ready to leave China if it became clear that their invest-ment could not succeed in the short term. Another shortcoming is that data were based on interviews with managers mainly at manufacturing firms, instead of other firms in services, entertainment, and other emerging sectors. Indeed, field-work interviews were not able to cover managers working for SME companies, which account for the vast majority of Korean business activities in China.

Notes

1 United Nations Conference on Trade and Development, Bilateral FDI Statistics.
2 For more details, see http://news.chosun.com/site/data/html_dir/2012/01/17/2012 011700055.html.
3 For details, see www.hankyung.com/news/app/newsview.php?aid=2015033044501.

References

Ito, Takatoshi and Chin Hee Hahn. 2010. The Rise of China and Structural Changes in Korea and Asia, KDI.
Jung, Jae-Ho .2011. The Emergence of China and the Future of Korean Peninsula. Seoul: SNU Press [in Korean].
Lee, Kwang-Jae. 2012. Asking on China, Seoul: Hakkoje [in Korean].

Lim Hyun-Jin and Hae-Ran Lim .2013. East Asian Cooperation and Community, Seoul: Nanam [in Korean].

Moon Jung-In. 2010. Asking the Future of China, Seoul: SERI [in Korean].

Peng, Mike W., and Yadong Luo. 2000. "Managerial ties and firm performance in a transition economy: The nature of a micro-macro link." The Academy of Management Journal 43(3): 486–501.

SERI (Samsung Economic Research Institute). 2004. Chinization and the Future of Korean Economy.

Shin, Gi-Wook and Joon Nak Choi. 2015. Global talent: Skilled labor as social capital in Korea. Stanford University Press.

Shin-Huang Michael Hsiao. 2014. "Political Risks in Doing Business in China: Comparing Foreign Business from Japan, South Korea, and Taiwan." (Second Workshop Presentation on Political Risk and Human Mobility, Jeju National University, March 18–19).

Sonoda Shigeto, Jang Hong-Keun, Park Joon-Shik. 2014. "A Comparative Fieldwork Study on the Korean, Japanese, and Taiwanese Multinational Managers as a Significant Factor of Global Corporate Competition in China." Korean Regional Sociology 15(3).

Index

Page numbers in **bold** denote tables, those in *italics* denote figures.

Printed in the United States
by Baker & Taylor Publisher Services